Love and Blessings

Avatar Adi Da Samraj

LOVE and BLESSINGS

The Divine Compassionate Miracles of
Avatar Adi Da Samraj

VOLUME ONE

compiled and edited by Bill Gottlieb

THE DAWN HORSE PRESS
MIDDLETOWN, CALIFORNIA

NOTE TO THE READER

All who study the Way of Adidam or take up its practice should remember that they are responding to a Call to become responsible for themselves. They should understand that they, not Avatar Adi Da Samraj or others, are responsible for any decision they make or action they take in the course of their lives of study or practice.

The devotional, Spiritual, functional, practical, relational, and cultural practices and disciplines referred to in this book are appropriate and natural practices that are voluntarily and progressively adopted by members of the practicing congregations of Adidam (as appropriate to the personal circumstance of each individual). Although anyone may find these practices useful and beneficial, they are not presented as advice or recommendations to the general reader or to anyone who is not a member of one of the practicing congregations of Adidam. And nothing in this book is intended as a diagnosis, prescription, or recommended treatment or cure for any specific "problem", whether medical, emotional, psychological, social, or Spiritual. One should apply a particular program of treatment, prevention, cure, or general health only in consultation with a licensed physician or other qualified professional.

Love and Blessings is formally authorized for publication by the Ruchira Sannyasin Order of Adidam Ruchiradam. (The Ruchira Sannyasin Order of Adidam Ruchiradam is the senior Cultural Authority within the formal gathering of formally acknowledged devotees of the Divine World-Teacher, Ruchira Avatar Adi Da Samraj.)

Copyright © 2006 The Avataric Samrajya of Adidam Pty Ltd,
as trustee for The Avataric Samrajya of Adidam.
All rights reserved.
No part of this book may be copied or reproduced in any manner
without written permission from the publisher.
(The Dawn Horse Press, 10336 Loch Lomond Road, #305, Middletown, California 95461, USA)

The Avataric Samrajya of Adidam Pty Ltd, as trustee for The Avataric Samrajya of Adidam, claims perpetual copyright to this book, to the entire Written (and otherwise recorded) Wisdom-Teaching of Avatar Adi Da Samraj, and to all other writings, recordings, and images of the Way of Adidam.

"Adidam", "Da Plastique", and "Fear-No-More Zoo" are service marks of
The Avataric Samrajya of Adidam Pty Ltd, as trustee for The Avataric Samrajya of Adidam.

Produced by the Avataric Pan-Communion of Adidam
in cooperation with the Dawn Horse Press.

International Standard Book Number: 1-57097-185-4
Library of Congress Catalog Card Number: 2006920458

CONTENTS

INTRODUCTION   11
"Instant Everybody"
The Eternal Love and Infinite Blessings
of Avatar Adi Da Samraj
by Bill Gottlieb

Places, People, Practices, and other special terms   28
mentioned in *Love and Blessings*

PART I   31
Respite and Recovery

A Gift of Life on New Year's Day   33
my eleven-year-old niece's miraculous recovery
from a skiing accident
by Margaret Dickow

The Guru as Refuge   38
the Gift of heart-freedom during cancer
by Denise Getz

Eyesight and Insight   51
healing my vision and my feeling-heart
by Jannie Martinus

The Thunderclap   54
my sudden disease—and Sudden Help
by Gary Ryan

Remember and Never Forget Adi Da Samraj   59
my Divine Guru saves my son's life after a
devastating car accident
by Mark Stewart

No Complications   86
my successful brain surgery
by Bob Kunz

He Saved My Life   91
the miraculous reversal of a medical crisis
by Tom Williams

The $4000 Wheelchair   95
a sudden and unexpected change in the lives
of my father and mother
by Rick Evans

Ward 11   98
my father's miraculous recovery from pneumonia
by Raewyn Bowmar

PART II   107
Touching the Troubled Heart

Sacred Hair   109
overcoming my obsessive-compulsive disorder
(trichotillomania) by Grace
by Rachel A. LaMell

Relinquish Your Tendencies by Turning to Me   116
devotion as the True Cure for my chronic anxiety
by David Rosen

The Cherry Farm   125
freeing my son from heroin addiction
by Francine Conrad

A Box of Chocolates and a Loaf of Wonderbread   128
Divine Instruction and Blessing in transcending
an eating disorder
by Elaine Gruenke

PART III   137
Protection from Harm

    Thank You, Beloved Adi Da Samraj   139
    the Divine Blessing of a soldier in Iraq and his family
    by Algernon E. Crawley Sr., Patricia Battle-Crawley,
    and Algernon E. Crawley Jr.

    "See to It They Are in a Safe Place"   152
    Avatar Adi Da Blesses my ill father, my mother, and me
    by Debra Hibbs

PART IV   161
Business and Blessing

    The Divine Medicine   163
    Avatar Adi Da Blesses my health clinic
    by Louise Darragh-Law

PART V   173
Guidance for Children

    A Place to Be with Him   175
    Blessings for my daughter, Adara
    by Laura Ballance

    Serene Passing   183
    my seven-year-old daughter's trust in
    Avatar Adi Da Samraj
    by Sheriden Vince

    My Self Is in My Heart   188
    my son's remarkable relationship with
    Avatar Adi Da
    by Karl Kaiser

PART VI   197
Divine Intervention in Death

"You're Already in Ecstasy!"   199
my father's Blessed death
by Daniel Green

A Relatively Good Day   209
the easy death of my friend
by Antonina Randazzo

The Doctor's Prayer   216
my mother's death transition,
Blessed by Avatar Adi Da
by Ulla Brust, MD

I Am in a Very Good Place Now   219
profound Help and Blessing during my husband's
nine years with Alzheimer's disease, and during his death
by Eileen Mulvihill

Requesting the Compassionate Blessing of Avatar Adi Da Samraj   229

AN INVITATION   233
Become a Formal Devotee of Avatar Adi Da

ABOUT THE EDITOR   247

"I Work on the Pattern that is Invisible, Prior, not yet observed—and then I Breathe it down into the world."

—Avatar Adi Da Samraj
1996

INTRODUCTION

"Instant Everybody"

Avatar Adi Da Samraj
The Mountain Of Attention Sanctuary, 2005

"Instant Everybody"

The Eternal Love and Infinite Blessings of Avatar Adi Da Samraj

by Bill Gottlieb

> *By Means Of My Avataric Incarnation here, I Have Given you My Divine Secret.*
> *My Divine Secret Is This: I Am <u>Eternally</u> Present, and I Am <u>Omni</u>-Present. . . .*
> *I Love you Now.*
> *I Will Love you every "then" and "there".*
> *And I <u>Always</u> Loved you (and every one, and all, and All).*
> *That Is How I Got To here (and every "where").*
>
> —Avatar Adi Da Samraj

This is a book of stories—about human need and Divine Response.

This is a book of testimonials—about mortal suffering and Miraculous Intervention.

This is a book of devotion—to a Person whose sympathy is so great, not only does He <u>Love</u> everybody with unqualified, unobstructed feeling, He literally <u>became</u> everybody: comprehending all, embracing all, suffering all. And declaring, from His Universal Heart, I <u>Am</u> humankind.

This is a book about humankind. About a soldier in Iraq, a woman going blind in Holland, a man on his deathbed in California, and how they—and many more suffering human beings like them—asked for and received the Love and Blessings of the Eternally Present and Omni-Present Divine Avatar, Adi Da Samraj.

A Morning of Blessings

It is early morning at Adidam Samrajashram—the Hermitage Ashram and principal residence of Avatar Adi Da Samraj, on the remote island of Naitauba, in the Republic of Fiji. Sea turtles swim inside the reef, Pacific pigeons coo in the trees, and thousands of dew-drenched hibiscus flowers—red, yellow, and peach-colored—bloom on hundreds of bushes.

In an office on the side of a steep hill is a woman who has just picked dozens of those flowers. She is a devotee of Avatar Adi Da Samraj and she is helping to organize the morning requests for His Blessing.

She carefully re-reads the letters of request from each devotee, written on behalf of himself or herself, or on behalf of a family member or friend. She double-checks to make sure that she has received via email a digital photograph of every person involved in each request. When she is satisfied that all is in order, she prints out the letters and photographs, puts them in a folder, and, carrying the folder and a basket of flowers, walks down the hill to a wide lawn bordering the ocean, and then on to a suite of offices.

She is quiet, respectful, intent—she is next to Aham Da Asmi Sthan, the home of her Divine Guru, Adi Da Samraj.

On woven Fijian trays, she prepares the requests for presentation, one by one. She places the photos on the trays and offerings of flowers around the photos.

Once the trays are finished, she carries them to the Glass Pear, the office of Avatar Adi Da. Then she enters an adjacent room, where two bowls stand on pedestals—they are marble bowls, covered with gold and silver leaf, and were gifts to Avatar Adi Da from His devotees, in gratitude for His Blessings. She fills each bowl with fresh water and carries them into the Glass Pear, putting them next to the trays. This is the water that Avatar Adi Da will use in His mysterious baptism of Blessing.

The devotee then presents the day's requests for Blessing to Ruchiradama Quandra Sukhapur Rani, for her final review. She is the representative of the Ruchira Sannyasin Order—the order of formal renunciates who have consecrated their lives utterly to Avatar Adi Da and His Way, and who are the sacred cultural link between Avatar Adi Da and His devotees. Ruchiradama Quandra Sukhapur works in detail with every request, ensuring that each one is rightly prepared as a sacred offering to Avatar Adi Da Samraj. The requests are also reviewed by Avatar Adi Da's personal physician, who provides Him with a detailed medical report with each request for Blessing that involves a death transition, illness, accident, or other physical difficulty.

Then, when Avatar Adi Da is ready, the trays and bowls are taken into His room by Ruchiradama Quandra Sukhapur. She sets the bowls before Him on a table that devotees have constructed specifically for the morning Blessing. And, one by one, she and the doctor read to Avatar Adi Da the letters of request, and answer any of His questions regarding the exact nature of the individual's circumstance. The trays are put before Him—trays with a photo of a devotee about to have surgery, or a devotee's mother who has had a stroke, or a devotee's son who has been in a car accident.

And Avatar Adi Da Samraj—His human body infused in every cell by the Conscious Light that is the fundamental substance of existence, His universal presence of Conscious Light surrounding and pervading all, His transcendental identity of Conscious Light utterly beyond space and time—responds at Heart to these suffering people, and Compassionately Blesses them.

Dipping His hands into one of the bowls, He douses the photos with water, anointing them again and again.

He may perform "laying on of hands" on a photo, touching a body part that a letter has indicated requires healing.

He may place a flower on that area—or cover the entire photograph with flowers.

He may rearrange the photos, as He did for a devotee's eleven-year-old niece who was severely injured, surrounding her photo with the photos of her family, then moving His hands in slow circles above them.

Avatar Adi Da extends His hands—and, universally aware, universally active, universally present, He extends His Divine, Compassionate, Miraculous Blessings.

He does this every morning when He is residing in Fiji at Adidam Samrajashram . . . or when He is residing at the Mountain Of Attention or Da Love-Ananda Mahal or Tat Sundaram, His Hermitage Sanctuaries outside of Fiji . . . or when He is residing anywhere else in the world.

And, as you will read in some of the stories in this book, Avatar Adi Da sometimes performs laying on of hands not only on a photograph of a person far away, but on the body of a person nearby—hugging someone, placing His hand gently on a heart or a head, or gently stroking a face.

He has said this of His Blessing-Process:

I begin each day by receiving requests for Blessing from devotees. Their requests are sometimes relative to difficulties of their own, such as health problems, or other matters. Sometimes they are requests for Blessing on behalf of people to whom they are somehow related. I am always given pictures of them. And something is said to Me about whatever is the problem, and what is actually being requested.

This is what I do at the beginning of each day—give My Blessing-Regard to people and conditions of various kinds, using a visual association. I extend Myself through this Regard profoundly—I Intervene, I participate in the conditions in which people are suffering. And My Blessing does purify. It can be integrated with conditions in such a fashion that conditions are changed in various ways. This is how I Work.

—March 15 and September 9, 2004

The Miracle of the Heart

The Force of Real God pours out of My Body all the time. It never stops. I am full of all space-time. All Love-Bliss and all the marvels of Divine Being are in My Being. All miracles are potent in My Heart.
—Avatar Adi Da Samraj

The stories in *Love and Blessings* are "Leelas", a word from the ancient, sacred language of Sanskrit, meaning stories about the Incarnate Divine Person and His enchanting Divine "Play" with His devotees and all beings. The statement that Avatar Adi Da is the Incarnate Divine Person is made by His devotees on the basis of their heart-recognition of Him.

This recognition is not a static belief or rote dogma. It is both a heart-felt certainty and a process, a responsive devotional practice of attentive turning to the Divine Heart-Master, and grateful conformity to His Heart-Word of Instruction. It is a direct and wordless recognition that Adi Da Samraj—the One to Whom they devote themselves—is not some kind of "Creator" or Divine "Parent" or "Representative" of God. Adi Da Samraj is the human Incarnation (or Avatar) of the Divine Reality That is Always Already the Case—the Conscious Light that is the "Source" and "Substance" of all apparent arising forms, the only Real God.

It is that One who mysteriously and paradoxically and Compassionately Blesses beings in and as Avatar Adi Da Samraj. And the key to understanding the Leelas of the Divine Compassionate Miracles of Adi Da Samraj is to understand and feel Who the Divine truly is, and what He has Avatarically Incarnated to do.

I am not Calling you to believe that I Am the "Creator-God"! I am Calling you to recognize and understand My Avataric Divine Revelation of Myself As the Revelation of What God Really Is—Guru, the Divine Liberator, the One and Only and Non-Separate Reality.
—Avatar Adi Da Samraj
Aham Da Asmi

Avatar Adi Da's Divine Leela is told, in happy gratitude, by His devotees. They want you to have the opportunity to experience what they experience: the Miracle of Living Truth, Blessing their lives. They want you to know about and consider the way of life that Avatar Adi Da offers: The Way of the Heart, or the Way of Adidam. It is not a life of seeking <u>for</u> experience or for "God", but of present-time communion <u>with</u> the Divine Conscious Light in Person. It is the moment-to-moment, devotional relationship with the Radiant, Free, Love-Blissful, Divine Guru, Adi Da Samraj.

The Divine Compassionate Miracles of Adi Da Samraj are, however, not only about achieving positive human change. Avatar Adi Da teaches that the fundamental cause of suffering is <u>seeking</u> for a change of state—for more pleasure or less pain, for power or progress, for mystical experience, for <u>any</u> earthly or heavenly goal. This is because seeking reinforces the <u>seeker</u>, the "I" who experiences whatever is positive or negative, the "I" who is inherently limited, mortal, and suffering. The Way of Adidam is about transcending the seeker, and Awakening, by Grace, as Reality, as Conscious Light in which the seeker appears and disappears. Avatar Adi Da calls for the understanding and transcending of <u>every</u> motivation—including the motivation to see or experience a miracle!

In a passionate, serious, and humorous conversation with a group of His devotees in His early years of Teaching, Avatar Adi Da explored the conventional idea of miracles—why human beings feel they need to see a miracle in order to be convinced of and respond to the Greater Reality, and why miracles, in and of themselves, are never sufficient to cause a human being to devotionally surrender his or her life to the Divine:

AVATAR ADI DA SAMRAJ: You haven't received enough Revelation yet? Do you need to see a really big, miraculous vision or something? What is it you need? What would be really impressive? Perhaps I should be present just in a body of light that looks substantial but which you can put your hand right through, so that no matter where I go, everybody will always be saying, "Hey, look, my hand goes right through it!" People swatting at My Body no matter where I go, just to test it out and go, "Wow!"

What do you need? What miracle would you like to see performed? It would have to satisfy you, you see. It would have to prove something to you. What do you need? If I were standing here in My twenty-five-foot flaming fire-body, you would be falling on your knees, you know what I mean? You wouldn't have any problem about surrendering. You would surrender yourself completely if you were confronting such a vision directly.

What do you have to see? What will you worship? What is the Revelation that makes you surrender spontaneously? You can imagine some manifestation or other of a Spiritual nature that would oblige you to surrender spontaneously. Other phenomena of experience allow you still to maintain some quality of ego-possession, a lack of surrender. So, what do you have to see in order to surrender?

Is surrender the result of something that makes you comfortable? Can anything <u>create</u> surrender, or does everything delay it—everything, including wonders and miracles? Each of these is just another distraction, an experience in itself. You might work yourself up to a little release in the face of it, but that confrontation cannot create the release.

What you need is a big miracle—if only so that you will realize that miracles are not sufficient, and that you are going to have to surrender in the face of things just as they are. That kind of surrender cannot be caused, but perhaps you need to see the big miracle to find that out.

You think true surrender is caused by some dramatic confrontation—a "miracle". You hold on to this popular idea of salvation—that you would be a perfect saint if only you had the perfect vision.

The Compassionate and Liberating Work of Avatar Adi Da Samraj

On September 10, 2004—the thirty-fourth anniversary of His Re-Awakening to His Divine Self-Nature in 1970*—Avatar Adi Da Samraj spoke to His devotees at Adidam Samrajashram and worldwide (via the internet), and responded to their questions. After hours of discourse, He began to speak about His mysterious Blessing-Work with all beings, explaining how it was made possible by His Divine Self-Realization—by His Re-Awakening as Conscious Light, the fundamental Identity of existence.

What I Do all day requires an extraordinary sensitivity to countless beings, which I suffer without limitation. I could not Do the Work I Do if I were not suffering It. My Blessing-Regard is moved by this suffering, by this complete absence of illusions. To be most profoundly Awake intensifies the awareness of the suffering nature of the world to a virtually unbearable degree—if there were not the Awakening that accompanies It.

You could not even look at what I see. You could not bear it. It is an exquisite suffering, an unlimited suffering that spreads Me all over the earth. Therefore, you cannot want This, but you can grow into It and Realize It. And Realization is not what you think—it is What you <u>Are</u>.

The instant My early Work was done—the instant, in 1970, that I Re-Awoke to My Divine Self-Nature—I was "Meditating" all.† Not even a day off! Not one. Instant everybody. And now My experience has been "everybody" for thirty-four years.

Of course, this is <u>My</u> Work. It will not be the same for others who are Divinely Self-Realized by My Grace in the Way of Adidam, for they do not have My Avataric Work. But it will be the same in that there is this sensitization, this transformation from desire to compassion, this unqualified sense of the suffering nature of all beings.

—Avatar Adi Da Samraj
September 10, 2004

---

*The story of Avatar Adi Da's Life is fully recounted in His Spiritual Autobiography, *The Knee Of Listening* (Middletown, Calif.: The Dawn Horse Press, 2004).

†For a description of Avatar Adi Da's "Meditation of all", please see chapter 17 of *The Knee Of Listening*.

If you talked to several devotees of Avatar Adi Da about why they became and are His devotees, they might mention one or more of Avatar Adi Da's many attractive qualities. His spontaneity and freedom. The breadth and brilliance of His Teaching. His persistence in working to Divinely Awaken His devotees. His perfect integrity. But a quality that every devotee would no doubt mention is Avatar Adi Da's <u>Love</u>—His obvious Compassion for and Heart-embrace of any and every person He encounters.

His Love is obvious—in His eyes and His gestures, in His words and His silence, in His Life and His Work. He is the Incarnation of Love. And He Incarnated because of love.

Avatar Adi Da says the impulse that initiated His Avataric Incarnation—and specifically, the moment in His Life, at the age of two, when He first fully identified with His human body-mind—was sympathy and love. It was triggered in relationship to a puppy His parents had given Him:

As a Conscious "creation", or by-Me-Embraced condition, "Franklin Jones" began one day while I was crawling across the linoleum floor in a house my parents had rented from an old woman named Mrs. Farr. There was a little puppy, which my parents had gotten for me, running across the floor towards me. I saw the puppy, and I saw my parents. The "creation" of "Franklin Jones" began from that moment. All of the rest of the events that occurred during the two or more years before that moment were not the years of "Franklin Jones". He had no existence before that time, which was the Conscious (or Intentional) beginning.

The reason for this gesture was a spontaneous motivation associated with a painful loving of the people around me. It was not merely compassion for them, as if they were poor people I could help. It was a painful emotional and physical sensation in my heart and in my solar plexus. It was profoundly painful even then, and it always has been. It was associated with the full knowledge that these people to whom I was committing myself were going to <u>die</u>, and that I would <u>die</u>. I knew that if I Incarnated in this life-form and circumstance, if I became this body and its lifetime, I would also die its death. And I knew that, as this bodily incarnate being,

I was, in due course, going to be separated from every one and every thing I loved in its lifetime. This was all fully obvious to me—and, yet, this spontaneous gesture, this painful loving, this profound sensation, awakened in me and moved me into the body, animated me physically. Thus, it was, altogether and simply, a sympathetic response that brought me into the sphere of human conditions, and of gross conditions altogether. That response was identification with mortal existence, but it took place by means of Delight. In that Exaltation, the wound of mortality was forgotten. Thus, it was not the noticing of mortality, in and of itself, that generated my Movement into this plane. Rather, it was the Love-Response, the attracted Response, in which all of the negative aspects of gross conditional existence were effectively forgotten—in Love, in Delight, in Love-Bliss.

—Avatar Adi Da Samraj
The Knee Of Listening

Avatar Adi Da's Divine Sympathy is, in a sense, twofold.

It is Divinely <u>Compassionate</u>: His constant Intention and Work are to help alleviate the suffering of countless beings.

And it is Divinely <u>Liberating</u>: His constant Intention and Work are not only to reduce the possibility and consequences of suffering, but to Awaken all beings beyond suffering into the unlimited Happiness of <u>Real</u> God—the perfect peace and searchless satisfaction of Conscious Light.

But, even though Avatar Adi Da is Conscious Light Itself, Avatarically Incarnate, neither His Compassionate nor His Liberating Intention is automatically fulfilled.

The Realizer's Mere Existence Serves the World

from a Talk given by Avatar Adi Da Samraj
on July 29, 1980

DEVOTEE: Beloved Master, does Divine Self-Realization always involve entering into an active Teaching-relationship with people in order to transform them?

AVATAR ADI DA SAMRAJ: No, Realization (of any degree) does not necessarily involve active service in that sense. But compassionate service is inherent in Realization Itself. The Realizer's mere existence serves the world, because he or she is effective in the subtler dimensions of existence. Therefore, the mere existence of a Realizer has an effect on world events, on people's states of mind, on all kinds of things, although that effect may not be sufficient to bring about complete Enlightenment in the world—obviously that has never happened, even though there have been many Realizers of various degrees. The Realizer's service is based on his or her mere existence. The Realizer is not obliged to negative, dissociative states of being, clearly, but whether or not he or she actively serves through participation with others is another matter. Such active service depends on the qualities of the individual Realizer and the circumstance that arises around that one.

My Work as Divine Avatar does not necessarily require an intent to change the world, any more than the "radical" nature of the practice of the Way of Adidam involves an intent to change the body-mind. But the inherent relationship to the world or the body-mind that is Divine Self-Realization is inherently transformative. It releases forms of attention or contraction. It is, therefore, a siddhi (or power), the Great Siddhi.

The presence of a God-Realized individual is inherently liberating. Realization liberates that one first of all, and then the Realization itself becomes a liberating effect on others. ∎

Avatar Adi Da Is the Liberator, Not the "Good Luck" God

There are causes and there are effects. There is free human action and its results, or what is sometimes called "karma". Avatar Adi Da Intervenes in karmas, and His Blessing-Influence can—and often does—change a situation for the better. But, as He has Revealed, He is <u>not</u> the proposed "Creator-God", with ultimate power over beings, capable of changing any and all destiny at will. He is not the "good luck God", who bestows hoped-for good fortune, like a good job or good health. That idea of "God"—as a Parent-Deity who sometimes responds (and sometimes doesn't) to the pleas of His children—is a myth, a desperate belief, generated and elaborated throughout the world by human beings in our suffering and bewilderment. Ultimately, the conditional realm of time and space, of cause and effect, is an infinitely complex, ever-changing, mysterious maze of mortal destiny. Avatar Adi Da has called it a "fistful of dust"—and He is not a magician, changing dust into Light. He is the Liberator, Awakening beings <u>beyond</u> dust, into their prior identity <u>as</u> Light:

I make My Compassionate Gestures, but it is simply My Nature to Do so. My Fundamental Work is relative to the process of Realization.

—Avatar Adi Da Samraj
July 20, 2004

And that Liberating Work is also not an automaticity.

If I could simply sit in My room and Enlighten the whole world by three o'clock this afternoon, I would be happy to do so. But it does not work that way. There is a necessary transformative process that you must engage. And I have Revealed it to you.

—Avatar Adi Da Samraj
July 20, 2004

The basis of that transformative process, Avatar Adi Da says, is being fundamentally <u>disillusioned</u> with the temporary satisfactions and inevitable dead ends of conditional existence, and therefore intensely and passionately <u>purposed</u> to the Freedom of Divine Enlightenment.

Avatar Adi Da has spoken of His own serious process, or "sadhana", of Divine Re-Awakening:

In this Body there has never been a day, a breath, a moment, wherein the Great Matter of Divine Realization was not <u>the</u> matter of profound importance. All the terribleness and inevitabilities in mortal life were immediately clear to Me, and felt most profoundly.

Fear and suffering were immediately, tangibly obvious to Me and experienced by Me, from the earliest days of My Life. And so everything that has to do with Ultimacy has been <u>the</u> matter of importance of every moment of My Life.

For the serious person—the truly serious person—that is the way it is.

It is not that you become serious when you are associated somehow—yourself or some relation—with illness and bad luck. Every moment is serious to the extreme, because of the nature of bondage to conditional existence.

—July 20, 2004

In other words, Avatar Adi Da is saying that the same experience and motive that bring people to Him for His Compassionate Blessing—the experience of fear and suffering, and the motive to be free of that—would, if fully felt, motivate a person to come to Him for His Liberating Blessing. In fact, He has even compared non-Realization to illness:

Non-Realization is the worst cancer in the universe. It is the worst sickness. It is the most horrific disease. Its implications cover the entirety of everyone's life. The world is filled with its symptoms and reeks with its torments and potentials, coming from all directions, most of which people cannot even see.

—July 20, 2004

If non-Realization is so horrific, why would you or anyone else not be interested in Realization?

Speaking frankly and fiercely as the Divine Liberator, Avatar Adi Da explains very clearly why this is:

People are immune. Their patterns of body-mind keep them immune. Their self-indulgent habits keep them immune. Their distractedness with the various things of life and desire make them immune. Their lack of discrimination. Their inability to understand what is going on. Their complete unavailability to understand what is going on. Their naïve presumptions. Their virtually infinite capacity to accept lies and be diverted by deadly nonsense. People do not know they are unwell.

—July 20, 2004

The Way of Adidam—the Yoga of the devotional relationship to Adi Da Samraj as Divine Guru, chosen because you are disillusioned with ordinary life and feel the need for His Liberating Blessings—is the Way that plainly acknowledges that you are unwell. And it is also the Way to be made well again—now, and in every moment of recognition of and response to Avatar Adi Da Samraj, the "Divine Medicine that cures the heart".

Many people don't even know there is an alternative, that there is any way beyond conditional existence, or they think conventional religious offerings are sufficient.

I have made the Way of Truth, of Reality, the Way of True Divine Self-Realization, completely available. I have Revealed It in Its totality. That is what I am here for.

—Avatar Adi Da Samraj
July 20, 2004

Divine Self-Realization—Realization of Reality, of Conscious Light, of the Ultimate Nature of Existence—is the ultimate import of Avatar Adi Da's Miraculous Compassionate Blessings, and of the stories in this book.

It is a heartbreaking book—about the burden of suffering and death, and the Avatarically-Given Gifts of Freedom and Eternal Life.

It is a book of stories by joyous, grateful people—people in love with, and Loved by, their Divine Guru, Avatar Adi Da Samraj. They have written these stories to communicate to you something precious and unique about His Love and His Blessings—which are given to everyone and everything. It is a miraculous book offering you a miraculous possibility—the joy of present-time communion with the Incarnate Divine Person.

Avatar Adi Da is the Divine True Lover in the universe. He calls everyone to Himself—to the deathless, fearless Freedom, Happiness, and Peace beyond the body-mind. That is the nature of His Divine Person and Work—the Person of True Love, the Work of True Blessing.

Places, People, Practices, and other special terms mentioned in *Love and Blessings*

This book was created in the context of a living culture of practitioners and a sacred way of life. Therefore, some of the words used by the various contributors to designate places, people, and practices are unique to the Way of Adidam that Avatar Adi Da Samraj has Revealed. The words are used to preserve the reality of the contributor's lives, as lived in relationship to Adi Da Samraj. We offer these brief definitions of the words and terms to aid your appreciation of the stories.

Avatar Adi Da's Names and Titles

Avatar—One who has "crossed down" from the Divine to the manifest world.

Adi Da—the Original Giver, the One Who Gives.

Love-Ananda—the One Who is Love-Bliss.

Samraj—the Divine Sovereign of the heart.

Adidam Samrajashram—Adidam's principal Hermitage Sanctuary, the island of Naitauba, in Fiji.

Communion Hall—a place devotees of Adi Da Samraj establish, by installing a photographic Image of Adi Da Samraj, for meditation and sacramental worship.

cooperative culture—the practice Avatar Adi Da's devotees engage of living and cooperating with other members of Adidam for the sake of intensified practice and mutual "expectation and inspiration".

Da Love-Ananda Mahal—Adidam's Hermitage Sanctuary in Hawaii.

Darshan—sacred devotional sighting of Adi Da Samraj.

Devotional Prayer of Changes—a practice given by Adi Da Samraj of prayerful communion with Him for the sake of positive change in life-circumstances and the world.

Divine Image-Art—The Art-Work created by Avatar Adi Da Samraj, especially His Art-Work created since 1999. Avatar Adi Da has worked with the camera as a technical means, using photographic negatives as "blueprints" for the fabrication of monumental art-forms. For information about the Transcendental Art-Work of Adi Da Samraj, please visit www.daplastique.com.

intimate partner—a term Avatar Adi Da's devotees use to describe their "significant other", whether or not legally married.

laying on of hands—in the Way of Adidam, a practice given by Adi Da Samraj of invocation of Him and His Blessing for the sake of physical healing through touch.

Leela—a story of the "Divine Play" of Adi Da Samraj.

The Mountain Of Attention Sanctuary—Adidam's main Hermitage Sanctuary in northern California.

Murti—a representational Image of Adi Da Samraj (generally a photograph of Him).

Prasad—anything that is given to the devotee by Avatar Adi Da Samraj, as a tangible expression of His Blessing.

prostrate/prostration—a full extension of the body on the floor or ground, in devotional surrender to Adi Da Samraj.

puja—sacramental worship and invocation of Adi Da Samraj, in a bodily active form, including waving lights and incense, washing and anointing an Image of Him, offering flowers, and so on.

"radical"—Avatar Adi Da uses the word "radical" to mean "gone to the root", rather than the conventional meaning related to politics.

Real God—Avatar Adi Da and His devotees use the term "Real God" to indicate that they are referring to That "God" Which Is Reality or Truth Itself, not a conventional theistic idea of "God".

Ruchira Avatara Bhakti Yoga—the fundamental practice of Adidam: moment-to-moment devotional turning of the four principal faculties (of body, emotion, mind, and breath) to the Ruchira Avatar, Adi Da Samraj.

Ruchiradama Quandra Sukhapur Rani—one of Avatar Adi Da's senior renunciate devotees, a member of the Ruchira Sannyasin Order.

Ruchiradama Nadikanta—one of Avatar Adi Da's senior renunciate devotees, a member of the Ruchira Sannyasin Order.

Ruchira Sannyasin Order—the collective of Avatar Adi Da's senior devotees, and Adi Da Samraj Himself, who have legally renounced all property and devoted themselves entirely to Spiritual and Divine purposes.

Satsang—the Company of the Divine Master, Adi Da Samraj.

"Source-Texts"—Avatar Adi Da's Avataric Divine Wisdom-Teaching is given in His "Source-Texts", which are the summary books of His Writings and Discourses designated as part of His Eternal Message to humankind.

Sukra Kendra—the Temples at each of the Hermitage Sanctuaries reserved for Adi Da's use in His Work of Divine World-Blessing.

Tat Sundaram Hermitage—a small Hermitage Sanctuary in northern California.

turn/turning to Adi Da Samraj—"turning" to Adi Da Samraj is a simple description of the primary practice of the Way of Adidam, which is also called "Ruchira Avatara Bhakti Yoga" (see above).

Way of Adidam / Way of the Heart—two Names for the Way of the devotional and Spiritual relationship to Adi Da Samraj, which He offers to all beings.

"My Work in Response to any apparent devotee is beyond personal. It is a connectedness to everyone."

—Avatar Adi Da Samraj
August 28, 2004

PART I

Respite and Recovery

A Gift of Life on New Year's Day

*my eleven-year-old niece's miraculous recovery
from a skiing accident*

by Margaret Dickow
Northern California

It was early in the day on New Year's Eve—December 31, 2003—when my brother Charles called me. He said that my brother Peter had just called him from the emergency room at a hospital near Lebanon, New Hampshire, where Peter and his family had been on a skiing trip. My niece, Kimberly, had been in a serious accident.

On Kimberly's first run down the mountain, she apparently lost control and headed into a grove of trees next to the slope. Her father saw her go whizzing by at breakneck speed and skied down after her. When he got to the bottom of the run, he saw a group of people gathered around someone lying next to a tree. It was Kimberly—with her head split open, bleeding profusely. She was airlifted to a nearby hospital and rushed into the trauma room. The doctors were unable to give my brother any hope that she would live through the night. The "best case" scenario, they told him, was that she would survive but be completely paralyzed or have severe brain damage.

I got off the phone and I immediately started to remember and invoke Avatar Adi Da and request His Blessings in a feeling-prayer—that this sweet eleven-year-old girl be allowed to live, and not find herself a paraplegic or worse for the rest of her life.

I called Adidam Samrajashram—where my Divine Guru was residing at the time—and relayed the message of my niece's condition to Indigo (the devotee responsible for submitting requests for Beloved* Adi Da's Blessing) and to my son, Jonah, who was there on retreat.

Indigo called me back and asked me to email photos of Kimberly and her family, and to immediately write a letter to Avatar Adi Da about Kimberly's situation. I felt that I had not a minute to waste. But I also felt very strongly that my Beloved Guru already knew of this situation and was Present there, with Kimberly and her family. This was so clear. It was also clear to me that surrendering the situation into His hands was my only possible gesture and responsibility.

After I sent the photos (which took several hours to locate since they had to be digital, and this was New Year's Eve, and my family was in the midst of a crisis), I stayed up to watch a video of a recent devotional sighting, or Darshan, of Avatar Adi Da. And I continued to stay up, all night long, as awake as I have ever been, with all my attention on this link between Avatar Adi Da and my niece, unconscious in a hospital room on the East Coast. It seemed that there was no time or space separating any of us.

INDIGO: It was late at night and I was hesitant to disturb Avatar Adi Da. I tried to convince myself that Kimberly would live through the night and that I could send the request for Blessing in the morning, when Avatar Adi Da usually received them, and all would be well. But I was also seized by the strong intuition that Kimberly would <u>not</u> live—that this girl needed the greatest Help

---

*Avatar Adi Da's devotees sometimes refer to Him as "Beloved", acknowledging the love and heart-intimacy of the Guru-devotee relationship.

possible, and she needed it <u>now</u>. In my deepest heart, I was certain that Avatar Adi Da was the One Who could help her most, whether she lived or died, that medical science could only deal with the physical body, while Avatar Adi Da could Influence the body, the psyche, the entire "package" that was Kimberly. He alone would know—and Do—what she needed in that moment, what would be most beneficial and auspicious.

It was 11:00 PM. I took a deep breath and printed the photographs that Margaret had sent of Kimberly, Peter, Jonah, and herself. I placed them on a tray, along with the letters from Margaret and Jonah prayerfully requesting Avatar Adi Da's Blessing for Kimberly. I also gathered flowers—as many as I could find with my flashlight at that hour of night.*

Then I called Ruchiradama Quandra Sukhapur (a member of the renunciate order of devotees in the Way of Adidam) to tell her about the situation. She asked me a few questions, and then agreed that the request for Blessing should be taken immediately to Avatar Adi Da's house.

In the kitchen of His house, I talked to Jacqueline, the devotee who was attending to Avatar Adi Da that night, telling her about the need to ask for His Blessing for Kimberly. Looking over the tray to make sure that everything was in order, she entered Avatar Adi Da's private quarters.

I waited in the kitchen for about ten minutes until Jacqueline came out. She looked overcome with astonishment at what had occurred. She told me that Avatar Adi Da had instantly stopped what He was doing and received the request. He rearranged the photographs on the tray, putting Kimberly in the center, and the photographs of her father, her Aunt Margaret, and her cousin Jonah around her. (Margaret had not been able to find a photo of Kimberly's mother on such short notice.) He then placed His hand an inch or two above Kimberly's picture for a moment, and started moving His hand in a slow, clockwise motion, as if to move the loving energy of Kimberly's family in towards her. Avatar Adi Da

---

*The flowers that accompany a request for Blessing are a devotional offering to Avatar Adi Da. He frequently uses these flowers in His Work of Blessing, sometimes placing a flower on the part of an individual's body (in the photograph) that most requires healing, sometimes even covering the entire photograph with flowers.

did this for some moments, then started the process all over again, holding His Blessing hand over Kimberly, and then waving His hands in the same clockwise motion. Then He sent the tray into His Sukra Kendra, the Holy Temple reserved for His use, where He goes every day to do His mysterious Work of world-Blessing.

MARGARET: When Indigo called me and told me of Avatar Adi Da receiving the tray of photographs and prayers for Blessing, the light in the room where I was became "Bright" with His Presence. She said the tray went into His room one minute after midnight, Fiji time. This struck my heart so profoundly—that His very first action of the New Year was to Bless a little eleven-year-old girl who was in a perilous position. Words cannot express the gratitude that I felt—and also the certainty that Kimberly would be fine.

I spoke to my brother several times the next morning. He said that Kimberly had briefly opened her eyes, which everyone felt to be a good sign. And he also said that—"miraculously"—the huge swelling of her brain that the doctors had been monitoring, and that they were very worried about, had not only stopped but was reversing itself. The doctors said that in brain injuries like Kimberly's it usually takes days, if not weeks, for this to occur. The reversal astounded everyone who was treating her.

I told my brother of Avatar Adi Da's Blessing, and he was so truly thankful.

The doctors had thought that Kimberly might have to be in the hospital for a long time, perhaps months. But she was released from the hospital in a little over a <u>week</u>. This is a hospital where they treat the worst ski injuries from Vermont and New Hampshire, so they see a lot of traumatic head injuries. My brother told me that the staff was amazed that the long-term swelling and all the other effects of this type of injury had not even happened. The staff at the hospital said more than once that her speedy recovery was "a miracle".

Within a few weeks, she was back at school. Brain scans showed no permanent damage.

I spoke to my brother Peter today—May 19, 2005—to wish him happy birthday. Kimberly is completely well, with no signs of trauma. Once again, he expressed his gratitude and thanks to Avatar Adi Da. And my heart breaks when I remember this utterly Compassionate Blessing from my Beloved Guru, who so directly touched and healed this little girl.

The Guru as Refuge

the Gift of heart-freedom during cancer

by Denise Getz
Northern California

In November 2002, I traveled to Hawaii to join a team of Avatar Adi Da's devotees working on the digital development of His Divine Image-Art. At the time, Avatar Adi Da was living in Hawaii, at His Hermitage Ashram, Da Love-Ananda Mahal.

For me, this was a dream come true. I loved doing this work and hoped to be able to permanently relocate in Hawaii, to serve my Guru. However, I had some personal business to attend to before I could move. And so, in late December, I returned to my home in northern California. A couple of weeks later, I had a medical checkup for what I thought was a cystic problem with one of my breasts. The doctor was concerned and asked me to see a specialist. I left the appointment feeling very vulnerable and afraid.

When I arrived home that night, there was a small package on my desk. I opened it, and inside was a beautiful rudraksha bead on a silver chain. (Rudraksha beads are round, intricately grooved, brown seeds from a tree that grows in India and throughout Asia. They are often used as prayer beads.) It was a Gift from Avatar

Adi Da, Who had given a similar Gift to all those serving the process of His creation of His Divine Image-Art.

I wept in gratitude and immediately put it on. I wore it nearly every day for the next year-and-a-half. It would be a touchstone of my relationship with my Beloved Heart-Master, Adi Da Samraj, and a constant reminder of Him.

A few weeks later, in January 2003, I was diagnosed with breast cancer. Just six months before, my regular doctor in California had given me a clean bill of health. Two or three weeks after that exam, an enormous mass of hardness appeared in my left breast, but it did not occur to me that this could possibly be cancer.

When I was told that it was, I was so shocked that I felt paralyzed. And I became immediately terrified that I would die soon—the size of the tumor was quite daunting, and I feared the worst.

My first impulse was to ask Avatar Adi Da for His Help.

I wrote to Him that evening, and included a medical report that provided as much detail as I knew about my situation and prognosis.

A day later, I was told that He had received my letter and medical report and had sent me His Love and Blessings. He asked me to keep Him informed of my progress "every step of the way". I was so deeply grateful for His Help and His Blessing.

I went through a week or so of testing to determine the size and type of tumor, and whether it had metastasized to other parts of my body. These tests included manual exams, blood tests, biopsies, x-rays, and an MRI.

These were some of the most difficult days of my life.

I was told I had a much better chance of recovery if the cancer had not spread—but not knowing whether it had or not was utterly terrifying.

I noticed that my mind raced everywhere in fear, and that my only peace was to sit in meditation and turn to Avatar Adi Da. I could even feel happy in this turning to Him, in the midst of this difficult circumstance. I was deeply impressed with the fact that I did not feel prepared to die—that even though I had been a devotee of Avatar Adi Da and a practitioner of Adidam for more than two decades, the fear of death was overwhelming my mind and heart.

The day that I was to find out whether or not the cancer had spread was one of the hardest days of my life. I remember feeling that I might go insane with fear.

For hours in the early morning, before my appointment with the clinicians, I held the rudraksha bead given to me by Avatar Adi Da to my heart, my chest, and my breasts, and I prayed for His Help and Intervention.

After a time, I felt a shock of Energy enter my body. It was very strong, and felt like it had sucked all the energy of my chest, heart, and breasts, all the energy of the cancer, into itself, into a point, into nothingness. It is hard to describe the sensation, but it was very strong, and I felt that all the energy of the cancer had been contained and was no longer spread out from the tumor. This was an extremely moving and powerful experience, and it calmed my heart. I found out a few hours later that the cancer had not spread. And I began the ordeal of recovery.

It was recommended that I undergo chemotherapy. I have always been the type of person that doesn't even want to take an aspirin, so this was a difficult decision to make. But both my allopathic and naturopathic doctors felt this was the right approach, so I accepted their advice and decided to proceed with the treatment.

Again, this was so frightening to go through. As one of the chemotherapy infusion technicians told me, "If it's strong enough to make your hair fall out, it's strong medicine." And about three weeks after the first treatment my hair did fall out. I felt it die, and then it began coming out by the handful. I went to a local hairdresser and, with tears and determination, asked her to shave my head. This was quite a strange experience, and more traumatic than I expected. I felt naked and cold. Friends and family sent me scarves and hats.

Every three weeks I had another chemotherapy infusion. After each of these sessions, I wrote Avatar Adi Da a letter thanking Him for His Help, asking for His Blessing, and including a current medical report. After receiving each letter and report, He sent me His Love and Blessings.

Before this illness, I had never directly and verbally received my Divine Guru's Love and Blessings: this was an extraordinary Gift. I always felt calmed and helped, and His Regard gave me courage to face the very difficult effects of the treatments each week. I wore the rudraksha bead every day, and regarded His photograph during the chemotherapy treatments, to keep my attention focused on Him, and not on the fear and discomfort of the treatments.

About three weeks after the first treatment, I was given another MRI, as part of a study I was participating in. I was told that there was already a significant reduction in the size of the tumor. After the third treatment, my doctor examined me and was totally amazed—the tumor was 70 to 80 percent gone! She was very surprised and pleased by these results, and I was elated.

But she also let me know that I would still have to undergo a mastectomy in order to remove the last of the tumor. Losing my breast was difficult to imagine, but I was determined to get through this difficult process, no matter what.

A profound advantage of going through this ordeal in the era of the internet was being able to see Avatar Adi Da regularly, in live occasions of devotional sighting that were broadcast from Adidam Samrajashram. To see Him almost every day, and to feel and receive His Blessing-Regard during these occasions, helped me so much to turn my attention to Him, and not become collapsed in depression or fear. Avatar Adi Da's Darshan was literally a lifeline for me.

After four chemotherapy treatments, it was time to have another MRI. There was still a mass in my breast, so I knew more treatment was needed. But I was ill and weak from the chemotherapy, and wished profoundly that the ordeal would end.

After the MRI, my doctor literally waltzed into the treatment room and announced that I would not need a mastectomy after all. The MRI could no longer detect the tumor—because it was gone! The mass in my breast was nothing but a fluid-filled cyst.

I wish I could adequately describe the joy and elation I felt at receiving this news. I hugged my doctor and intimate partner and wept in relief. I will never forget this moment. I have an indelible image of white flower petals blowing in the breeze, as I walked outside after being told the tumor was gone.

I am told that having a tumor completely disappear after chemotherapy is rare. My naturopathic doctor thought that it was a miracle. In fact, he thought my allopathic doctor must have made a mistake with her original diagnosis! All my friends and family were amazed. I was so happy to immediately write to Avatar Adi Da with the news. I feel certain that His Blessing-Help was the miraculous intervention that made this outcome a reality.

However, the ordeal continued. I underwent a chemotherapy treatment which had been scheduled for later that same day, with a new chemical agent that made me extremely ill. (My doctors wanted me to complete a full course of chemotherapy, even though the tumor was gone.) I spent the next month in bed in a lot of pain and almost immobile, and then decided to discontinue chemotherapy. My surgeon recommended I undergo an "excisional biopsy" to see if there was any microscopic evidence of the cancer in the breast or the lymph nodes, and I reluctantly agreed to this surgery.

I asked Avatar Adi Da for His Blessings again, for the positive process and outcome of the surgery. He received my photograph, my letter, and a gift of flowers. A couple of hours before going to the hospital, I received this message from a member of the Ruchira

Sannyasin Order (the order of Avatar Adi Da's formal renunciate devotees):

> *Beloved Adi Da Laid His hands on Denise's photograph and on her flowers, for her biopsy tomorrow morning, 10:00 AM Wednesday. He sent His Love and Blessings to her. He said something very interesting. He said, "How long is this going to go on?" And I said, "Beloved Master, You've healed her. This should be the last one hopefully." So He is ready for Denise to be reintegrated in a full life of service and devotion in the culture of devotees and not have to go through this anymore. It was really clear. He said it very sweetly. After saying that, He Laid His hands on her flowers.*

I was profoundly grateful for this Gift of His Blessing-Regard. I knew then that the ordeal was over, by His Grace. I went to this surgery with Adi Da's Blessings, and I knew that they would not find any cancer. Right after the surgery, my surgeon told me that she could not find anything, and a week later the lab results came back, confirming that there was no cancer at a microscopic level in my breast tissue or lymph nodes. The doctors were once again amazed at this outcome, and I was released to heal and become strong again.

It took me nearly a year to feel strong enough to go on a meditation retreat at Adidam Samrajashram, to see my Beloved Guru and express my profound gratitude to Him at His Feet.* At the end of June 2004, I traveled to the Fijian islands, staying for two nights on the island of Taveuni.

The night before traveling by boat to Naitauba, as I prepared to go to bed, I took off the rudraksha bead Gift from Avatar Adi Da, which I had worn daily, steadily, since the beginning of this ordeal. It sort of fell off my neck, into my hands, and I saw that the clasp on the chain had broken suddenly. Even though I am a jeweler by trade, I had no tools to repair it, and there was no place to purchase a new chain before getting on the boat the next

---

*The Feet of the Guru are traditionally understood to be a special point of devotional contact for the devotee, potent with the Guru's Blessing. Thus, devotees of Adi Da Samraj often use expressions like "bowing at His Feet" in heart-gratitude for His Divine Gifts.

morning. I knew that Adi Da's Gift to me had been with me all through this ordeal, and that now that I was going to His Ashram the next day, this period of my life was over. I wept in amazement at the perfection of His Gifts and His Care.

I wrote the part of this story you just read after the retreat in Avatar Adi Da's Blessing Company in July and August of 2004.

Even though there was some underlying anxiety (as probably all cancer patients have) about the possibility of a recurrence, I assumed that this ordeal was completely over. And so it was very shocking to find a lump in the same breast in October 2004—and then to find out that the cancer had returned. This time, there was a strong recommendation that I should have a mastectomy immediately.

The night I was told that the cancer had returned was extremely difficult. I was very afraid and my mind raced in every direction, seeking for comfort. I couldn't fall asleep and by early morning I was exhausted from mental agonizing.

At a certain point that morning, by Grace, I just sort of gave up. I acknowledged that this situation was not controllable by me, and I turned my attention to my Heart-Master, Beloved Adi Da.

Suddenly, I felt as if I was collected to His Heart and then lifted up into a dimension of energy and feeling in which I "saw" the matrix or grid that is mind. I saw that mind simply exists, that experiences of mind (and body) are created by touching the grid of mind with the faculty of attention, and that thought and experience follow attention.

I saw and felt that there is an automaticity that is mind and thoughts—but that is not "me". I knew that I am not the struggle, the fear, or the mental agony of having a serious disease. I am free. I am free to "touch" that grid at any point, or not. I am free to turn my attention to Avatar Adi Da in any moment, rather than helplessly follow the pattern of thoughts and fears that seemed to be programmed into this "experience". And, in that turning, in that moment, there was Avatar Adi Da, "Bright" as Love and Light, completely obvious to my heart—and my heart-need.

The Grid of Attention

from a Talk given by Adi Da Samraj
on August 15, 1995

AVATAR ADI DA SAMRAJ: You can think of attention as being an unmoving point on a grid—a grid of infinite size, made of horizontal and vertical lines, and (thus) made of an infinite number of possible points. If attention appears to "move" or is willed to "move", so to speak, it is actually the grid that moves. The point of attention is always the same. The point of attention never moves. The grid apparently moves—and, thus, attention is apparently shifted to another point on the grid. That point coincides with the object of attention at any moment.

Fundamentally, then, in terms of the mechanics of attention, that is all there is—this point of attention and the grid, which is the field of apparently modified Energy, taking on the apparent form of objects (or points) in space-time. In terms of the mechanics of experiencing, there is the unmoving point of attention, and the apparently moving grid, associating attention with different modifications of Energy, moment to moment. Therefore, in Truth, there is neither attention nor the grid. There is simply Consciousness Itself and Its Inherent Radiance.

Attention and the grid, or attention and any apparent object, is the conditional form of the Ultimate. Even though there is only this grid and this apparently fixed point of attention (speaking in conditional terms), you perceive it to be objects and spatial conditions and temporal conditions, and so on—all these pictures that you call the "world" and "experience". But all of that is just an illusion, made by this apparently fixed point of separate attention and this mechanical grid, and something like that is what is going on in the brain. *(continued on following page)*

When you are seeing objects, you imagine that you are looking into an objective space, but the mechanism that is showing you visual objects is this brain intermediary. And the visual cortex functions very much like I just described—just a kind of Energy-grid that associates the fixed point of attention with apparent visual modifications of Energy. If you were not identified with the body—and, therefore, with a spatial concept of your existence—all you would see would be this grid.

What is the grid, ultimately, anyway? It is just an illusion, or a conditional representation of Consciousness Itself, Which is One with Its own Energy. In conditional terms, attention is one with its every object. There is no "difference" between Consciousness and Energy. And, therefore, there is no "difference" between attention and its any object. Don't you know?

There is no "difference" between attention and any object.

There is no "difference" between Consciousness Itself and Its own Energy.

There is no "difference" between Consciousness Itself and any "thing" that appears to arise.

There Is Only One Absolute Condition. ∎

The Guru as Refuge

I understood what is meant in traditional scriptures when they describe the Guru as "refuge". This was an utterly ecstatic revelation. I jumped out of bed, and immediately went to write to Avatar Adi Da and thank Him for this Gift, this Revelation. I was so happy, and so utterly relieved. I wrote to tell Him of my medical situation, and again to ask Him for His Blessing and His Help, and to tell Him that I would turn to Him, and that I was not afraid.

This was such an amazing Gift. It made a deep impression on me, and gave me a strong impulse to cease to struggle with whatever was happening mentally or physically or emotionally, and to simply turn to Avatar Adi Da, which is the core of the practice in the Way of Adidam. I felt how my relationship to Avatar Adi Da is truly beyond the body and mind. I felt how <u>anything</u> can happen in this conditional world—but that it does not affect that heart-relationship with my Beloved Guru, Adi Da Samraj.

I had a mastectomy in mid-November 2004. Before the surgery and many times afterwards, Avatar Adi Da sent me His Love and Blessings.

Each time I would write Him to tell Him of my situation and my progress, He would give me His Regard, in the formal Way that He does: my photograph and flowers and letter were presented to Him, and He would douse them with Blessing water. These photos and often some of the dried flowers were sent to me as Prasad, a Gift from the Divine.

To open this beautiful packet of Prasad was so wonderful. I would feel Avatar Adi Da's Grace and His Love and Blessings, and see that my picture (printed on an inkjet printer) had been transformed into a watery mass of color from His water-Blessing.

In the weeks of recovery from the surgery and breast reconstruction, I would often hold one or more of these Prasad packets to my heart, and even sleep with them on my chest, and I would always feel comforted and helped.

I also asked Avatar Adi Da for His Blessing to be admitted as a patient to a clinic in New York City that I had discovered during my research into treatment options for cancer. I was intuitively certain that this was the right treatment for me. I had read that this particular doctor had many, many people wanting to be patients, and that only about one in five were admitted after a lengthy application process. I wrote my application, and was immediately accepted as a patient. I know this was another Graceful outcome of Adi Da's Blessing-Help to me.

The reconstruction of my breast did not end up working out very well. It did not look balanced and natural, and I wrote to tell Avatar Adi Da about this soon after the surgery, in addition to sending Him all the other medical information.

A few weeks later, Avatar Adi Da Samraj asked me what I was going to do about the reconstruction. I was surprised that He had asked about this, because it seemed to me to be rather mundane, and a matter of personal vanity only. But I wrote Him all the details that I knew at that time.

Within a couple of days, I received the most wonderful and humorous message from Him, in the form of a transcript of the conversation that He had with His physician, Charles, upon receiving my letter. He wanted me to know that it was completely okay to have this impulse to correct my appearance, and, in fact, that it would be good for me to have some positive outcome from this entire ordeal. I felt so profoundly relieved and loved by His compassionate, humorous, and loving communication to me. This occurred while I was still suffering the effects of the surgery quite a bit, and was the most healing and kind intervention. I was so grateful for this Help.

I feel very much changed by this ordeal and by Avatar Adi Da's Blessings. I no longer feel immune to death, as if I am immortal. I feel confronted by the reality of mortal existence every day, and it has sobered me quite a bit.

Avatar Adi Da has Helped me again and again. Through this whole process, I have felt more and more intimate with Him. At the time of the original diagnosis, I was weak in the practice of turning my faculties to Him, and rather childishly hoping to be cured and relieved of my situation. When the cancer returned I had to feel all of this again, and by the Grace of Adi Da Samraj's Help, I have became more capable of simply turning my attention, feeling, body, and breath to Him, rather than struggling with everything, seeking for relief, and wishing to be cured. It has become obvious to me that to turn to Avatar Adi Da in love is true healing—heart-healing—no matter what happens with my health, my life, or anything else.

After this story was written, Avatar Adi Da traveled to California and, in July 2005, Blessed Denise with His Touch during a Darshan occasion. She writes:

I have observed over many years of being a devotee of Adi Da Samraj that Leelas of His Divine Love and Blessing are truly <u>living</u>. Gifts that Adi Da gives in one moment of a devotee's life become ongoing features of life and of the relationship with Him. Telling the story of receiving that Gift is not telling about an event, but about a <u>process</u>. This is one among many signs of the timeless, eternal nature of the Guru-devotee relationship. And so my story has a new chapter.

In June 2005, Adi Da Samraj Graciously traveled to the Mountain Of Attention Sanctuary in California, to Bless His devotees and everyone. I was ecstatic at His arrival, having wished for a long time that I could be in His Divine physical Company again.

This became a wonderful period of many occasions of Darshan in His Blessing Company. On several of these occasions, Avatar Adi Da walked among hundreds of people, stopping again and again, to Bless every person with His Regard. One time, as He walked nearby, I became absorbed in devotional regard of Him, in love—and suddenly felt His hand on the top of my head! I was completely shocked—I had seen Avatar Adi Da Bless others in this manner, but had not imagined that He would Bless me with His Touch. My heart melted in love and gratitude as He placed His hand on my head in several places and gently Touched my face. His hand was cool and soft, and I wished that the moment would never end. His Touch was utterly loving and compassionate, and I felt a weight of suffering and separation lift from my heart. It was and is a completely generous and inexplicable Gift of Grace and heart-Intimacy.

I bow down to my Beloved Heart-Master, Adi Da Samraj.

Denise receiving the Blessing-Touch of Avatar Adi Da Samraj.
The Mountain Of Attention Sanctuary, July 2005

Eyesight and Insight

healing my vision and my feeling-heart

by Jannie Martinus
Holland

I am a sixty-five-year-old woman living near Amsterdam—and a devotee of Avatar Adi Da Samraj. Writing is difficult for me, especially in English. I tell this story—and I live my life—by the Grace of my Divine Heart-Master.

In the fall of 2003, I noticed that I could not see as well as I did before. Better glasses didn't help.

In the spring of 2004, the eye doctor diagnosed me with macular pucker in both my eyes: for various reasons having to do with aging, a thin layer of scar tissue forms on the macula, the center of the retina, gradually destroying vision. In my case, the illness was developing quickly, with progressive loss of vision occurring over weeks—even days. The right eye was worse. I could not read with it. The left eye was in the first stages of the problem.

I wrote my Divine Guru, Adi Da Samraj, and asked for His Blessing on my eyes—that the disease stop developing, that I may be completely healed in both eyes, and that I may be able to see clearly.

I also asked for His Blessing in allowing me to use this crisis to grow in the practice of Ruchira Avatara Bhakti Yoga—the moment-to-moment devotional turning of attention, feeling, body, and breath to Him. I intuitively felt that this last request was the most important.

Beloved Adi Da sent me His Love and Blessings. He Blessed my photo and that of my husband of forty-two years, who is not Adi Da's devotee.

The illness stopped—there has been no more loss of vision. I see the eye doctor, and I take medication for the problem. I know that I may need an operation in the future, but I am no longer afraid of losing my vision.

The illness stopped—and many other crises in my life started!

I am the devotee of the Divine Person, living in His precious human Lifetime. My husband is not a devotee. Needless to say, we have had conflicts about our priorities. The strange thing is, this has deepened our relationship and our love for each other, even though we don't know how it will ultimately affect our relationship. I know that Avatar Adi Da Blessed me <u>and</u> my husband—and this is the result.

My father died in WWII, when I was five years old. When he died, my mother lost her will to live—and died ten years later, of cancer.

Recently, I was in a shop and saw a clerk who was extremely sad because of the death of her husband a few weeks before. She had told me about the death in an earlier conversation. This time I did not speak to her—I did not want to. When I left the shop, tears were streaming out of my eyes—and I couldn't stop crying. From some deep level of my body the words surfaced, "She will not pull through." By Adi Da's Grace, I had the instant intuitive insight that I was re-experiencing my mother's sorrow, when I was five. I could not handle the sorrow then and had blocked my heart. On that day, the sorrow I had been carrying for six decades was released and relieved—by Grace.

I also felt that Avatar Adi Da answered my most important request for Blessing—growing me in my practice of Ruchira Avatara Bhakti Yoga. The moment I received His Love and Blessings, I could feel that He was offering me Great Help in my relationship to Him and my service to Him. I felt the deeply happy responsibility to devotionally turn to Him again and again and again, and that He had Blessed me to draw me to Him in profound heart-recognition and heart-response to Him.

Avatar Adi Da is carrying me to Him. I am doing things to serve Him that I would never have dared before, like organizing events to tell others about Him. My deepest longing is to bring Him new devotees—so that they, too, can experience the happiness of the relationship with the Divine Person. May you, the reader, through my story and all the stories in this book, recognize that the Divine Person is <u>here</u>, for you, to receive His Divine Blessings, His Divine Peace, His Divine Freedom.

I bow down at the Feet of my Heart-Master in surrender and gratitude.

The Thunderclap

my sudden disease—and Sudden Help

by Gary Ryan
New Zealand

My story begins on a sunny winter's day in June 2004.

I was out in the yard digging, constructing a small extension to my driveway. Suddenly, without any warning, I was struck by a severe, intense headache, or what is sometimes referred to as a "thunderclap" headache. The pain was so bad I was driven to my knees.

A short while later, I staggered inside to my room and lay on the bed, moaning in agony, as my intimate partner Merryl rushed in to see what was wrong. I described what was happening and she asked me several questions (she's a trained nurse). She was concerned that I might have had a small stroke, but I wasn't reporting or showing any stroke-like symptoms. Meanwhile, the pain continued unabated, and I lay there sweaty and nauseous. I took some painkillers, and several hours later, the pain had reduced slightly to a more bearable level. I fell into a disturbed and fitful sleep.

Upon waking in the morning the headache was still there but, on a scale of one to ten, the intensity of the pain was at five rather than ten. The origin of the headache was a mystery to me and to Merryl, as I had no history of migraines or any other kind of severe headaches.

The next three days I remained at home in unrelenting discomfort, unable to go to work. By the fourth day, however, the pain was reduced to a level where I could work. A couple of days later it had tapered off and was gone—much to my enormous relief.

Two days later I went to see my doctor and he referred me to a specialist. Two weeks after that, I was at the hospital for an interview. The specialist said that, although there were no obvious signs of neurological damage, I should have a CAT scan of my brain.

During the next two weeks, as I waited for the scan, my mind was filled with anxious thoughts as to what might be wrong with me. Did I have a brain tumor? Maybe I only had a few months to live? I felt very vulnerable, mortal, and afraid.

Two weeks after having the CAT scan I had another visit with the specialist. He informed me that the scan showed no signs of any bleeding but that there were some anomalies and that he wanted me to have an MRI. A few weeks after having the MRI, I received a letter for an appointment with a neurosurgeon at the hospital. I took Merryl with me for moral support as I had a feeling that the news was not going to be good.

Sitting in his office, we were informed that I had multiple brain aneurysms (weakened and bulging spots in blood vessels). Two of them were large, which meant they were prone to rupture—which can cause a hemorrhagic stroke! In the event of a rupture, the statistics told a grim story: in 25 percent of cases, the person dies immediately. Altogether, 75 percent are dead within two years. Because I had had multiple aneurysms, I was in the high risk range, with a 2 percent chance of a rupture every day for the rest of my life. If I chose surgical intervention to treat them, there was a 5 to 15 percent chance of some degree of brain damage.

Shaken and distressed, my intimate and I left the hospital, pondering what I should do next: live with the daily risk of a fatal stroke or undergo surgery and risk brain damage?

❖ ❖ ❖

Over the next month, the tension of this choice began to consume me. I had arrogantly assumed that I would live a long and healthy life, unaffected by serious injury or disease. What a shock to be confronted by my own mortality. Every day, as I awoke, my first thought was, "Is today going to be the day?"

Later, I was told that the previous manager of the engineering firm where I worked had died of a ruptured brain aneurysm at the age of forty-six (one year younger than myself). Obviously, this fueled my growing anxiety.

Stricken numb by the dilemma, unable to make a rational decision, I spiraled into a state of anxious depression.

❖ ❖ ❖

It was at this point that several of Avatar Adi Da's devotees from my local Adidam center contacted me and exhorted me to request the Blessings of Avatar Adi Da. And finally, after having felt weak in my practice for several years, I knew deep in my heart that they were right—I was in great need of Adi Da's Intervention and Blessing in my life.

A couple of days later, I sat down at the computer and wrote to my Divine Guru with my request for His Blessing.

About an hour later, I suddenly experienced a rush of feeling-energy enter and permeate my body, and I felt a strong connection to Avatar Adi Da. After the dark days of the last few weeks, this was wonderful.

For the next few days, at random moments during the day and in worship and meditation, this feeling would return and I would have a strong sense of being personally Blessed by Avatar Adi Da.

❖ ❖ ❖

About a week after requesting my Divine Guru's Blessings, I received a message from a devotee residing in Adidam Samrajashram. Avatar Adi Da had received the details of my medical condition and had sent "Blessings to Gary Ryan and his intimate partner."

He had Blessed our photographs, anointing them by hand with water, and had them placed in His Sukra Kendra.

I was profoundly moved by the Grace of Avatar Adi Da's personal Regard and I felt a depth of connection with Him that I had not previously known.

Over the next weeks and months the awareness of Avatar Adi Da's Compassionate Regard for my situation brought me great comfort and a release from my negative emotional state.

A couple of months later I returned to the hospital to undergo a cerebral angiogram, which would provide a detailed picture of the arterial structure of my brain. Although there was some risk associated with this procedure, I felt no anxiety as I turned to my Divine Guru.

After the procedure, still dozy from sedation, I caught a glimpse on a computer screen of a computer model of my brain's arteries. The largest aneurysm was clearly visible—and it was not a comforting sight!

I complete this account of my story a month after that procedure. My practice of Ruchira Avatara Bhakti Yoga—turning my attention, emotion, body, and breath to Avatar Adi Da—continues to grow and deepen. Simultaneously, I have felt increasingly uneasy about the risks involved in brain surgery. Many years ago I had major surgery on my lower back—and complications from that procedure kept me out of work for three years. So I am reluctant to undergo surgery again, especially when it involves such a delicate organ as the brain. Therefore, I have chosen to postpone surgery indefinitely unless there is a significant change in the size of any of the aneurysms, which will be monitored by an annual brain scan.

By the Grace of Avatar Adi Da Samraj, this experience has taught me that my relationship to Him—to the Divine Being in human Form—is the most important part of my life. Avatar Adi Da is the greatest Help that any person can have. Even the fear of my own mortality is insignificant when I turn to Him and receive His Divine Gifts. Secure in His Compassionate Regard, I will continue to resort to my Beloved Guru, whatever the future brings. I bow at His Feet in loving gratitude for His endless Grace.

Remember and Never Forget
Adi Da Samraj

*my Divine Guru saves my son's life
after a devastating car accident*

by Mark Stewart
Portland, Oregon

In the early hours of November 10, 2001, I was awakened by a phone call from my daughter, Chele. I immediately sensed something was very wrong, and my heart sank when she told me that the police had just knocked on her door to tell her that her brother Michael had been in a "horrible car crash", and had been taken by ambulance to the hospital in "extremely serious" condition.

I was flooded with adrenaline, but calmly asked her to meet me at our company offices so we could drive to the hospital together. I ran to my car, started driving, and then got on the cell phone to the hospital emergency room.

The nurses at the hospital couldn't tell me much. They said there had been a terrible accident and their emergency room was full of its casualties. They said they had been able to identify five of the six injured parties, and that the one they couldn't identify was "hanging onto life by a thread". This "young man" did not have any identification on him, and they said his face was so badly damaged he would be "unrecognizable". This confusing, frustrating, and terrifying message was repeated to me by three different nurses as I drove to meet my daughter.

When we met, we held onto the hope that the police that visited her had made a mistake—since the hospital couldn't tell us that it was Michael they were trying to save, we hoped there had been a horrible mix-up. After an agonizing hour-long wait in the emergency room, not knowing if we even had a reason to be there, a nurse came out holding a tennis shoe. My daughter collapsed, and as I caught her, I asked her, "Do you know for sure that this is Michael's shoe?" She just sobbed and nodded it was. I held her close and looked in her eyes and told her it was going to be okay.

We were taken immediately up to the waiting room of the intensive care unit (ICU) and doctors informed us of Michael's injuries.

A friend was driving Michael's car and he was a passenger in the front seat. As the car was crossing an intersection, another car came out of a side street at approximately sixty-five miles per hour and hit the passenger door head on. Michael had suffered massive facial damage. His nose and upper lip had been severed and were hanging by a small bit of tissue. His entire left eye socket and cheekbone had been crushed, and the bone between his eye sockets also had been crushed, basically splitting his facial structure into two pieces. The center bone was simply gone, they said. He had severe, deep cuts on most of his face. They made it a point to impress on us that his head had taken a massive blow, and that they feared and even expected brain damage.

He had two punctured lungs, broken ribs, a badly damaged spleen, a crushed pelvis, and his urethra had been severed and the bladder pushed up into his abdominal cavity by about twelve inches. He had a severe burn on his left leg as well. (These were the injuries that they knew about at that time.) They said they had given him fourteen units of blood and ten units of plasma and blood products and his blood pressure was still dropping. They suspected severed blood vessels and arteries in his trunk area. They also told us they had opened up his abdomen and repaired what they could, and that his abdominal surgery was still open.

As we absorbed this news, we were led into the room Michael was in and told to expect not to recognize him.

We entered the room and I saw my beautiful son, so badly damaged. I had never heard of or seen anyone so badly hurt who had survived.

His head was like a large round ball, with no features at all. His severed nose and lip were propped up into place, just for show I think, as the plastic surgeons had not been there yet. His left eye was dropped to the side and down. I remember mostly that his head was just so immensely huge and round and that his cuts were the most prominent feature.

He was completely invaded with dozens of needles and tubes. He had a tracheotomy and was on a ventilator that was breathing for him. There were about twelve trauma doctors and nurses present. My daughter later told me that the floor was completely covered in blood, but I don't remember seeing this at all.

Michael was completely unresponsive, but I went directly up to his head and began to speak into his ear. The first thing I said to him was that he should remember Adi Da Samraj by Name and by His face, and I told him to do nothing but relax and hold on to the feeling of Adi Da. I told him I loved him so very much and I told him he would be okay.

I have been a devotee of Adi Da since 1978 and, of course, both my children know about the Way of the Heart.* They also knew Adi Da directly, as He stayed at our home in 1998.

Michael and I had returned recently from a trip to Da Love-Ananda Mahal in Hawaii, where we had done architectural service and where Michael served in and around Adi Da's residence.

---

*The Way of the Heart is another Name for the Way of Adidam—the Way of the devotional and Spiritual relationship to Avatar Adi Da, which He offers to all beings.

We had one long conversation during this trip regarding the practice of whole-bodily turning to Adi Da and abiding in Divine Communion. We spoke about Who Adi Da really is, and I shared that Adi Da is Awake as the Truth and lives as the One, universal Being we call "God" or "the Divine". We talked about how the practice of turning to Adi Da realigns the body-mind and opens a door for Adi Da's most powerful Grace and Divine Intention to affect life and Awaken one to the Truth.

We also spoke at length about the practice of "self-Enquiry" that Adi Da Samraj has given, in the form of the question, "Avoiding relationship?"* I told him that my relationship to Adi Da and this practice He had given of self-enquiry had saved my life and matured me in ways I could not dream of.

At the hospital, I felt the best and only thing I could do for Michael was to remind him of what he already knew, and I told him again and again to remember Adi Da Samraj and hold His Name and His face in his heart constantly no matter <u>what</u> was apparently going on with his body.

This is all I spoke to Michael about, and I stayed by that ear for as long as I could, until the doctor finally told us we had to leave.

When we were leaving the room, Michael's trauma doctor calmly explained that he was not going to leave Michael's side for the next twelve hours. He said he had put all his other patients in the hands of other doctors, and he assured me he was the best trauma surgeon in the hospital. I asked him if he was fresh and rested, and he assured me he was.

He explained that usually in trauma cases there are one or two major problems that take careful management. He said Michael had at least five major problems, and to manage each one in concert with the others, while keeping Michael alive and stable, was

---

*The practice of self-Enquiry (in the form "Avoiding relationship?") spontaneously arose in the context of Avatar Adi Da's early Life, as a process of tacitly understanding the activity of self-contraction from Reality. The practice of self-Enquiry is given by Avatar Adi Da to His devotees not as a technique intended to achieve a specific result, but rather as a means to support the fundamental practice of Adidam, which is devotional turning (of body, mind, emotion, and breath) to Adi Da Samraj.

going to be very tricky. He told us that if Michael survived the next twenty-four hours, he would make it through in "some kind of shape" to eventual recovery. He told us to not expect him to ever be the same person mentally, if he survived. (At this point, the brain surgeons were standing by to relieve rising pressure in his brain.)

I asked him for brutal honesty, and he said he would give Michael a 50 percent chance of surviving the next twenty-four hours. We were then led back to the waiting room.

After consoling Chele, I went outside to get some fresh air. I got on the phone with my wife Debbie, Michael's stepmother, and told her the situation. I had not shed a tear up to this point, and I completely dissolved, sobbing and wailing to her on the phone. I was just overcome. She asked what she could do.

I told her to go into the Communion Hall (the place where we meditate, and where Adi Da had spent time when He stayed at our house), offer light and incense before the Murti (photographic Image) of Adi Da, repeat His Name, and put a photo of Michael on the altar, in front of Adi Da's Murti. I told her to then sit peacefully and visualize Adi Da before her and ask Him, in Michael's name, for His Intervention and His Blessing-Regard. She did this immediately.

I then called family and friends—and soon the waiting room was full.

As the hours passed, I was able to visit Michael between the preliminary surgeries on his face and his abdomen. (They continued to leave his abdominal cavity open, which struck me as odd and scary.) Every time I saw him, I reminded him to remember Adi Da.

At one point, as I was sitting at Michael's bedside practicing self-enquiry, I spontaneously began to move my right hand in a downward motion from the top of his head to just above the knees, holding my hand about six inches away from his body. I did this many, many times, as I continued to practice self-enquiry, and prayer, and remembrance of Adi Da.

After some time, I stepped back from Michael and observed above his body what I can only describe as heat waves, like sun off the pavement. This phenomenon was visible and obvious. At the same time, the solid objects in the room started looking less solid, and more liquid, and began vibrating.

I recognized this as a sign of the Spiritual Presence of my Beloved Guru Adi Da Samraj, and I spoke to Him and thanked Him for His Intervention and Help.

Michael's mother also mentioned seeing these "heat waves" on a separate visit that night. We had not talked at all until I passed her in the hallway to the waiting room and, while horribly upset and sobbing, she stopped long enough to tell me of these heat waves above Michael's body.

On my next visit to Michael's room, I was told that his major injuries were under some kind of control, but that his blood pressure was still dropping, in spite of the fact that he had been given several large transfusions. By this time, Michael's entire body had swollen to huge proportions, both from the fluids he was being given and the trauma to his entire person.

On this visit, as I prayed over Michael, I noticed that the "heat waves" above his body were now very definitely coming from <u>within</u> his body. As I put my hand above him, as I had before, a great force—a very strong force emanating from his body—pushed my hand away. I even tried to touch Michael's forehead gently, but the force pushed my hand back.

I wept deeply with gratitude, as it was obvious that my Beloved Lord was there, active and alive in my son. I thanked Avatar Adi Da for directly and Intentionally magnifying His Presence in Michael's body-mind, and I thanked Him for His Love. I found myself bowing to Michael's now Divinely-occupied body, and left the room.

By daylight the next day, it became obvious that Michael had severe disruption to his blood flow, in addition to the other major damage he had suffered.

The trauma doctor said they were assuming there were severed arteries in Michael's pelvic area, that this was a severe problem and a threat to Michael's life, and that they had to perform emergency vascular surgery in an attempt to arrest the loss of blood and blood pressure.

I immediately called my good friend and longtime devotee, William, who was living at Da Love-Ananda Mahal, and told him what was happening. William told me to call Dr. Charles Seage, Avatar Adi Da's personal physician. William also suggested that I take the time to write down what I could about the accident and Michael's injuries, and email a photo of Michael to Charles, for Adi Da to Bless.

I called Charles and told him what was going on. I asked if he could specifically let Adi Da know of the upcoming vascular surgery and the import of it. Charles listened carefully, asked a lot of detailed questions, and assured me he would get a report on Michael's condition to Adi Da.

Later, I was told that Charles took the report to Adi Da and that, as He read it, He put His hands on His Body in the locations of Michael's injuries. Charles said He then looked out the window and continued to address His own Body at these areas for quite some time. Adi Da then asked that I be sent His Love and Blessings, and He told Charles that He wanted to be kept informed of any changes in Michael's condition, as well as the time of the surgeries. I wept deeply upon hearing this.

The vascular surgeon was a young, confident doctor. He said he would find the severed arteries and fix them. He said that it might take an hour or so to find the exact problem and then it might take two to six hours to surgically repair it. He assured me he would do so without excess damage to important nerves in the sensitive groin area where he would be working. He did caution us, however, that damage to sexual functioning was a real risk.

As he was saying this, Michael was wheeled by, and I vividly remember the nurse manually squeezing the air bag that was keeping Michael alive and breathing during the trip to the operating room. I leaned down to Michael and again told him to remember Adi Da and not <u>ever</u> let Him out of his heart and mind. I kissed him on the hand and once again felt the force coming off the front of his body.

About seven hours later, the confident young surgeon came out with a huge smile and told me he "got it"—the two major arteries that serve both legs had been completely severed, and he had found and repaired them. Michael's blood pressure improved dramatically.

I gave the surgeon a big hug and a kiss on the cheek and high-fived him.

I called William and Charles immediately. Charles told me of Adi Da's remarkable response to the initial report, which I later found out He read about the same time as the repair work on the arteries began.

As they wheeled Michael out of the operating room, I leaned down, kissed him, told him I loved him so very much, and reminded him to <u>never</u> let the feeling, the memory, or the Name of Adi Da out of his mind and heart.

The force coming off his body was stronger than when he went in to surgery.

We were now about eighteen hours into the critical twenty-four-hour period after the accident. I was feeling some relief—and I was certainly feeling Adi Da Samraj.

The next great challenge was to stop the hemorrhaging in Michael's brain.

The neurosurgeons met with Chele and myself and told us that the CAT scans were showing increasing hemorrhaging, and that if this continued Michael would need emergency brain surgery. They had drilled a hole in Michael's head and installed what amounted to a pressure relief valve that would also be a starting point for surgery, if it became necessary.

By this time the roundness had gone out of Michael's head, and the plastic surgeons had done some preliminary stitching—

four hundred or so sutures to "hold things in place for a while". But there was a massive pooling of fluid in the back of his head—it was so swollen it looked as if a huge water balloon had been installed back there.

I called Charles again and spoke to him about the brain hemorrhage situation. The doctors were saying that if the next CAT scan showed <u>any</u> increase in the hemorrhaging there would be a huge problem, and Michael would have "severe brain damage" and require "dangerous surgery". I told Charles that the brain hemorrhaging had to stop, and I prayed over the phone that it would, and I asked Charles that he specifically inform Adi Da of this current development. Charles assured me he would.

The next CAT scan came back about two hours later. The doctor explained that it was identical to the previous scan. The swelling and hemorrhage had stopped.

He said that at first he thought he was looking at the previous CAT scan, and had to double check with the radiologist. He said that the hemorrhaging had definitely not gotten any worse and that this was a very good sign. He added that he almost <u>never</u> sees such an immediate reversal of that kind of condition.

Three more brain surgeons then joined us—just about the entire staff—and they said it was time to reduce the constant anesthesia for a minute and see if Michael could respond to their verbal directions.

Chele and I were there with them when they turned down the anesthesia, and they let both of us speak to him. Chele told him she loved him so much. I told him to remember and <u>never</u> forget Adi Da and to remember His Name, and I told him that Adi Da had personally Blessed him and his recovery. Michael nodded his head a tiny bit when I told him this, the first response he had made.

The doctors then told him he was in the hospital and asked him to lift up his left index finger. He did this promptly. Then they asked him to wiggle his left foot, which he did, then his right foot as well. Then they asked him to lift up his right index finger, at which point Michael lifted up his left middle finger. They looked worried, and I laughed before they again asked him to lift up the right index finger. I saw the slightest little smile on Michael's face, and told the doctors that he understood them just fine, and that he was messing with them a little bit. When I said this, Michael made the thumbs up gesture.

Then they asked him for a few more responses, all of which he made perfectly. They told us to say goodnight to him and they cranked up the anesthesia again.

The four doctors then took Chele and me into the hallway, and they all agreed, that based on these tests, they did not predict any severe brain damage. They said that somehow, some way, he had been spared brain damage. One of the doctors who had previously assured us Michael would be brain damaged just shook his head back and forth and finally said, "I don't have any medical explanation for the responses he just made, given the blow he took to the face and head, but I agree, he should be fine." They did caution us that it might take a few years before he was anything like normal. Chele and I were ecstatic. I hugged my daughter, and I went back into Michael's room to sit with him.

Between Chele, my wife Debbie, and myself, we were with Michael for every hour of the entire three weeks that he was in intensive care. We took three shifts and spent about thirty minutes at the end of a shift—every eight or nine hours—comparing notes, observations, concerns, and so forth.

By this point, I had photographs of Adi Da in Michael's room, and many of Adi Da's books and introductory pamphlets. I read for long periods from the books. I meditated and placed my hands on Michael and rubbed his feet, hands, and head. I constantly invoked Adi Da in that place.

We also paid constant attention to Michael's every move, need, and moment. We cheered up tired and stressed nurses and made sure we had the best nurses in that room. We were vigilant about Michael's care—and Adi Da was invoked all day and all night, for three weeks.

Michael's doctor now warned us of the next major hurdles.

Michael's abdomen remained open this entire time, covered only with a huge gauze pad just under the eighteen-inch incision. He explained that the swelling inside made it impossible and even life-threatening to close the incision. They would just have to manage with it as best they could, keeping out infection. They also had more abdominal surgery to perform.

In addition, there was the upcoming repair of the bladder and severed urethra. He explained that reattaching the severed urethra was hard enough but, in Michael's case, the bladder had been flipped upside down and traveled quite a distance up into the abdomen. This made arthroscopic surgery almost impossible, an opinion that was echoed by the urology resident that night. The doctors were convinced they would have to repair this area with open surgery, which would certainly severely damage sexual function. This was not acceptable to me, as I was counting on a complete recovery for Michael in all ways. I asked to speak to the chief of urology. This fine man assured me that he would personally make the arthroscopic attempt himself. He also assured me that he was a pioneer in this particular procedure and that he had complete confidence in his ability to make the repairs without the big open operation. He did say, though, that the real chance of success was about 30 to 40 percent.

I communicated all of this to Charles, who informed Adi Da Samraj.

The morning of this surgery, I was home and in the Communion Hall performing puja, a form of worship involving offering incense, candles, flowers—and the devotee's heart and life—to Beloved Adi Da, in His Murti Form. I found myself spontaneously putting my hands on the parts of Adi Da's Body that corresponded to where Michael would be having surgery. My hands went in top-to-bottom motions over the Murti of Adi Da, as I repeated His Name and did the Devotional Prayer of Changes,* always assuming success for the surgery and recovery for Michael.

---

*The Devotional Prayer of Changes is a form of Invocation of (and heart-communion with) Avatar Adi Da Samraj that is practiced by His devotees for the sake of positive changes in specific circumstances, whether personal or on a larger scale. (See also quotes on pp. 70–72.)

I got to the hospital and met the doctor just as he had finished the surgery. He was ecstatic and happily announced that he had completely reconnected the urethra and repositioned and repaired the bladder, all arthroscopically, without the invasive open surgery I had dreaded. He said it was very, very, very lucky that the operation went as smoothly as it did. He said the difficulty factor was a "ten"—but everything just fell into place and came together very easily. He said it was "stunning". Those were his words.

Draw on My Divine Virtue

from *My "Bright" Form*
by Adi Da Samraj

AVATAR ADI DA SAMRAJ: What is the practice I have Given My devotees for the positive changing of conditions? It is the Devotional Prayer of Changes, which is simply and primarily ego-surrendering and ego-forgetting heart-Communion with Me. In that heart-Communion with Me, My devotee actively relinquishes and releases all identification with and affirmation of negative (or non-useful) conditions, and My devotee actively affirms, receives, and enacts positive (or useful and right) conditions.

What is that process about? It is to make use of My Virtue, or My Mere and Blessing Avataric Divine Presence. In Communion with Me, you associate with, participate in, and draw upon My Divine Virtue.

Assume your responsibilities and thus really, effectively (rather than only randomly and, therefore, ineffectively), do the Devotional Prayer of Changes. Draw on My Virtue rather than bringing Me problems and negative conditions and expecting Me to deal with them. I have Given you the

Means for making positive changes, through your Communion with Me.

The Devotional Prayer of Changes can be effective relative to all kinds of things, if, as My devotee, you would draw upon My Virtue and do the Devotional Prayer of Changes as I have Given it to you—which is a form of Ruchira Avatara Bhakti Yoga, or devotional participation in My Blessing. By practicing the Devotional Prayer of Changes and (simultaneously) handling your responsibilities, you support and extend the kind of Work I have Done through the exercise of My Blessing-Powers.

You will always be able to draw upon Me, forever, through your right practice of the Devotional Prayer of Changes. After the death of This Body, I need not be physically present or present in any sense within the cosmic domain and intentionally exercising My Blessing-Powers.

I am here to show you the Way of inhering in Me and participating in Me, the Way that Grants you responsibility to provide the Mechanism for positive changes. . . . Your Devotional Prayer of Changes becomes effective because you use My Virtue, through your practice of Ruchira Avatara Bhakti Yoga, and through your taking your responsibilities seriously rather than imagining that they are only mysterious obligations that have nothing to do with you. You are drawing on My Virtue simply by practicing the Devotional Prayer of Changes, in the context of true Ruchira Avatara Bhakti Yoga. You allow your own mechanism to become the means.

My devotees are to provide the body-minds whereby My Divine Virtue becomes Effective. If you will really do so, then changes will occur. Yes, they will be changes that I have Made, but in the fashion I have just described to you. ∎

"True Prayer"

from *The Dawn Horse Testament Of The Ruchira Avatar*
by Adi Da Samraj

"True Prayer" Is Positive, ego-Transcending, and Fully psycho-physically Effective Prayer. If Prayer Is To Be Positively and Fully Effective, the Total body-mind Must Positively Change, At its Depth. That Is To Say, the mind (and, Indeed, The Total body-mind-Complex) Must Change—At The Conscious Level, The Subconscious Level, and Even The Unconscious Level.

Conventional Prayer Is A verbal (and egoic, or self-Contracted) Request To The mentally (and, Usually, Also emotionally) Presumed (Rather Than <u>Directly</u>, and Even <u>bodily</u>, Revealed) Divine. And conventional Prayer Is Uttered Under The Illusion (or With the idea and Feeling) That The (Very) Divine Is (Itself) Inherently and Necessarily Separate From the body-mind-self. But, For My Devotees, "True Prayer" Is Direct, ego-Transcending, and Total psycho-physical Participation In My (Avatarically Self-Revealed) Inherently egoless, and Self-Evidently Divine, Self-Condition (Which <u>Is</u> The Source-Condition Of all-and-All—and In Which every Apparent body-mind Is arising, changing, and passing away). . . .

By Truly Practicing The Only-By-Me Revealed and Given Way Of The Heart, Observe and Transcend The Process Of Ineffective (or Negatively Effective) and egoic (or Separative) Prayer, and Awaken To The Process Of True, Positively Effective, Really ego-Transcending, and Totally psycho-physically Participatory Prayer. ■

Next—about ten days after the accident—we were prepared for Michael's upcoming facial reconstruction. This surgery, which was scheduled and rescheduled about three times, would involve a heroic effort. Michael's plastic surgeon introduced herself to me about a week before the actual surgery. Immediately after the introduction, she pointed to a photograph of Adi Da and said, "Who is that man in the picture beside Michael's bed? It looks like someone I met in San Francisco in the seventies. What is his name?"

I told her it was Avatar Adi Da, and spoke a bit of what I knew of Adi Da's time in San Francisco, in the early seventies. She insisted that she was at an occasion of some sort with Adi Da and some of His "friends". She remembered the night as "hilariously funny".

I told her of Adi Da's highest Function (including His Divine Humor) and Who He in fact Is, and also told her that He had His direct attention on the upcoming surgery and on her as Michael's surgeon. She seemed pleased at this additional help, and offered her thanks for Adi Da's attention.

She then described what she must do for Michael—the incision from the top of one ear to the top of the other, the peeling off of the forehead and face down to the mouth, the bone repair, metal plating, and bone reconstruction, the reattachment of the inner workings of Michael's nose. She thought it might take five to six hours. She explained all the risks—blindness, nerve damage, and on and on. She asked me to sign a consent form, the first consent of any kind I had seen. I signed it, but I didn't initial all the risks she had disclosed. I told her that they had nothing to do with us and I would not acknowledge them with my signature. They would not happen. She smiled and said okay. I asked her if her life was going well, and if she was a happy person, and if she was having a good week. She assured me everything was fine and she was a well-balanced individual, and she looked forward to helping Michael.

Prior to the operation, I had kept Charles Seage and Avatar Adi Da apprised of Michael's situation, and continued with my constant vigil of prayer and the puja in the Communion Hall.

When the surgery finally came, it took eleven hours, almost twice what the plastic surgeon had predicted. We met her after the operation and she looked very happy with the results and very radiant, like she had just stepped off a cruise ship after a week's vacation. The first thing she said to me was surprising.

I wanted desperately to hear how it had gone, and I guess the look on her face was enough assurance, but I was stopped by her first words. She said that the operation had gone very well, but that the entire time of the surgery she could not get the image of Adi Da out of her mind. She said, "His face was in my mind's eye the whole time and it is still there now. Can you tell me why?"

I offered the explanation that Adi Da _Is_ Consciousness and, as such, that He is completely coincident with everything, and that in this instance His attention was deliberately and directly placed on her and the surgery. She nodded her head, said "That's awesome and please thank him," and went on to describe the surgery.

She had to build new bone between the eye sockets—all the original bone had turned to wet dust, like wet laundry soap, and had just disintegrated. The eye socket on the left was also destroyed in this way, and she built a new one out of a metal and bone compound. The cheek on the left also had to be rebuilt. She repaired Michael's nose as best she could, but said future surgery would be needed there. She said there was a lot of blood loss during the operation but Michael had stood up very well to the surgery and did not need the transfusions they had planned for. This was all absolutely fantastic news.

She remarked again that the image of Adi Da had not left her the entire time, and that it was unusual to work in this way.

These surgeries, and the others that followed, all had great risks, and a very narrow chance of complete success with no complications.

There was complete success and no complications—from any of the injuries or surgeries.

In particular, this plastic surgery presented incredible difficulties, which I read about later in the surgeon's notes. She described closing up the incision and the peeled-back face as "exceedingly painstaking and difficult", and that it "took great care and unusual effort to get it right".

In between surgeries, we held constant prayerful watch over Michael in intensive care. We became familiar with all the nurses and doctors, and very familiar with all of Michael's tubes, monitors, drugs, injuries, and details of care. On a daily basis, it seemed like thousands of things had to go perfectly right for Michael to recover.

In spite of a feeding tube, he began to lose weight—from a 6' 5", 200-pounder, to a 6' 5" 160-pounder. But it also became obvious that Michael was unusually strong—and had remarkable healing power. When a certain stage of recovery was expected, Michael would inevitably have signs of that stage two to three days early. This happened again and again. An example was his crushed pelvis.

There was talk among the doctors of the possibility of a large open surgery to repair the pelvis. They said the fractured pelvic areas were directly along the weight bearing lines, where surgery shouldn't be done. They said they would watch him for a week or so and decide later.

Well, during that week Michael oddly began lifting his knees up and draping one of his lanky legs over the side of the bed, and then retracting it again—sort of like he was doing abdominal crunches. To the surgeons, this demonstrated some healing, which was surprising—even more so, because his abdomen was still open, held together with only a large gauze pad. They decided that his pelvis would heal on its own.

After about ten days in the ICU, we looked forward to the five minutes or so each day during which Michael was taken off anesthesia long enough to be tested for responses, like moving his feet and hands. During these times, Michael was often very amusing.

When he awoke one time, he responded to all the commands except the last, where the nurse asked him to raise his left index finger—instead, he raised his left middle finger high into the air in her direction. I asked him if he liked that nurse, and he shook his head, <u>no</u>.

One time, as he came up out of the drugs, he looked off to one side and saw his girlfriend. One hand went towards her backside and the other up under her shirt. This was the day we knew he was going to be okay.

He was usually put in restraints during these times of awakening because, more than once, he grabbed for all the tubes that were keeping him alive and pulled a few out. I was stunned to see my daughter very calmly re-install the tracheotomy tube after Michael ripped it loose. I was the guy who guarded the catheter that would be our constant companion for the next six weeks, while the urethra healed.

The first time that Michael responded without prodding was about ten days after admission.

One of the nurses had asked what the book *Eleutherios*, one of Avatar Adi Da's Divine "Source-Texts",* was all about. She asked the question kind of loudly and Michael started waving his hand vigorously in her direction and raised his head up, toward her voice. He couldn't talk or open his eyes, but he waved and pointed. We tried reading what was left of his lips as he mouthed words. He was saying, "What's that?" as he pointed to the nurse and the book.

I finally figured out that <u>he</u> wanted to know what "Eleutherios" was. I explained that it was one of Adi Da's Names and the title of the book I had been reading to him. He calmed down, nodded his head, and gave the thumbs up signal.

He also became so loving during his moments awake. He would always gesture for kisses, and he would kiss you right on your lips every time—he would settle for nothing less. We would bend down to hug him and he would turn his head and give you

---

*The Wisdom-Teaching of Adi Da Samraj is gathered together, in its final form, in His many "Source-Texts", which He has designated as His Eternal Communication to humankind. In *Eleutherios*, which means "the Liberator", Avatar Adi Da describes the "Perfect Practice" of the Way of Adidam.

a big lip kiss, and mouth "I love you" all the time. All those kisses were on lips that had been ripped open, torn off, and reattached. The doctors later found a large piece of glass in his top lip. The one he kissed with.

Michael also became quite a thumb-wrestling champion. He liked to challenge us to thumb-wrestling matches at which he would sometimes cheat—and always win. Months later, Michael noticed his left thumb was a bit crooked and didn't match his right. x-rays revealed it had been broken in the accident and healed out of place during his hospital stay. One of the thumbs he would thumb wrestle with.

He was very strong as well. I would hold his hand for an hour or more at a time and he would often grip my hand and squeeze very hard the entire time.

Another uncanny part of his recovery: Michael would be out cold, but as Debbie, Chele, or I walked very quietly into the room he would <u>always</u> wake up, even when we were silent. He would wake up enough for a kiss and a handhold. Every time.

After the plastic surgery on his face and—finally—the closing of his abdomen, the doctors announced that "Michael was over the hump" and the rest of his recovery would be up to him. He would have a huge amount of work to do to recover, but they had done all the big surgeries and he had come out the other side.

So began a process of slowly waking him up more and more, explaining to him what had happened and where he was, and asking him to please, please stop grabbing at tubes. He was finally awake enough and had recovered enough that they began weaning him off the breathing machine.

Finally the day came when they took out the tracheotomy tube, covered up the hole in his throat, and asked him his name. My heart broke when I heard a faint voice from inside that big body.

He began getting a little stronger each day, and healed quicker then anyone expected. He eventually was moved to a rehabilitation hospital, where he spent three more weeks recovering.

❖ ❖ ❖

One of the first nights there, when he and I were finally alone with no nurses or doctors or friends, he asked me to please listen to some things he had to tell me.

He said that he knew he was alive because of something greater than himself, and that he thinks that was Adi Da Samraj.

He described his memory of four "nightmares" that he had during the previous weeks. (In every case, his nightmares corresponded to surgical procedures.)

The most graphic and haunting nightmare was that all of his blood had been removed and replaced. Another nightmare was that his head and whole body were being stapled up. He said that as each staple went in, he was trying to get to Adi Da, and the stapling kept bringing him back to the nightmare. He then asked me if I wanted to know how he was able to "wake up" and come back from these "nightmares"? I told him that, of course, I wanted to hear about it.

He explained that the only thing he remembers about coming back from the "nightmares" and the one thing that ended the nightmares" was asking, "Avoiding relationship?" . . . "just like we talked about, Dad." He said he used the enquiry "Avoiding relationship?" all the time now in the rehabilitation hospital, "just like I did before the accident happened." Michael had been experimenting quite a bit with the practice of self-enquiry after our discussion about it, during our visit to Da Love-Ananda Mahal.

He also requested that I be sure Adi Da's photograph was always in his view, all day long, and that I take all but one of Adi Da's books home, so he could focus fully on one at a time—when he finished one, I should bring him another. Out of all the "Source-Texts", he chose to keep *Eleutherios*—the word spoken loudly by the nurse after his second surgery, and to which he responded. (He, of course, had no memory of this.)

Eleutherios

from *Eleutherios*
(*The <u>Only</u> Truth That Sets The Heart Free*)
by Adi Da Samraj

Truth Is the Ultimate Form (or the Inherently Perfect State) of "Knowledge" (if mere knowledge becomes Truth-Realization).

Truth Is That Which, when fully Realized (and, Thus, "Known", even via the transcending of <u>all</u> conditional knowledge and <u>all</u> conditional experience), Sets you Free from <u>all</u> bondage and <u>all</u> seeking.

Truth Is Eleutherios, the Divine Liberator.

Real (Acausal) God is not the awful "Creator", the world-making and ego-making Titan, the Nature-"God" of worldly theology. Real (Acausal) God is not the First Cause, the Ultimate "Other", or any of the Objective Ideas of mind-made philosophy. Real (Acausal) God is not any Image created (and defined) by the religious ego. Real (Acausal) God is not any Power contacted (and limited) by the mystical or the scientific ego. Real (Acausal) God is not any Goal that motivates the social ego.

Real (Acausal) God Is Truth (Itself)—or That Which, when Most Perfectly "Known" (or fully Realized), Sets you entirely Free.

Real (Acausal) God Is Eleutherios, the Divine Liberator. ∎

He said to please tell Adi Da, "Thanks very much for His Help."

Out of nowhere, he also wanted to thank "Adi Da's doctor", who he was sure had been at the hospital the whole time. He hadn't been told anything of Charles' role in communicating with Avatar Adi Da, or even that Adi Da had a doctor. I told him that Charles Seage was a friend of mine, and Adi Da's doctor, and that he was in Fiji during the surgery. Michael still insists that he was at the hospital on and off the whole time and that he was still coming around "when he needed to".

I was humbled at Michael's will and intuition, and the awesome Grace, which his story suggested.

It is my feeling that these "dreams" were in fact experiences, and Michael's presence of mind to turn to Adi Da Samraj and to practice self-enquiry speaks volumes, not only about Michael's true heart, but also about Adi Da's unwavering effect on Michael.

This was what Michael had waited all day to tell me in private.

I still weep at the memory of my badly damaged child speaking these words as the first real conversation we had had for a month.

Michael's stay at the rehabilitation hospital was half of what had been predicted. We were told to expect six to eight weeks—he was home in less than three. His follow-up surgeries also went flawlessly, usually taking about half the time predicted.

Especially remarkable to me was the last visit with the neurologist in the rehabilitation hospital. He spent thirty minutes or so basically saying to us that, after extensive testing and therapy, they could find no evidence whatsoever of even the slightest brain damage. He went on to say that it is <u>very</u> rare for someone to absorb the blow that Michael did and not be permanently impaired in some way.

He ended the visit by saying: "Michael, you must have a direct link to God, because that is the only answer for your health at this moment."

Michael's specialists—from the trauma surgeon to the urologist to the plastic surgeon—routinely call in all the residents and nurses to greet Michael whenever he comes in for an appointment. He is a huge inspiration to all of them. He is a bright light in the midst of the pain and suffering and death they deal with every day. They almost all have promised him a chapter in their upcoming books, and they all in their own way speak of the "miracle" that he represents.

The surgery on his bladder and urethra was a complete success, far beyond his doctor's high expectations—he is completely healed.

His plastic surgeon almost wept when she saw him for the first time after his initial recovery from surgery. She smiled a huge smile, cupped his face in her hands, and told him everything was so magnificently healed she could not have prayed for more.

At one point, we began to prepare for the final, large surgery, which would further repair Michael's nose.

When the nose specialist initially met with Michael he made plans to go back into the eye socket area, rebreak what had been built and repaired, and apply new steel plates around the eye socket in addition to fixing the nose. He said the left eye looked a bit sunk in and that he thought he could improve it.

After that appointment we traveled to Tat Sundaram—a Hermitage Sanctuary in northern California—to do more architectural services for Adi Da in and around the area where He lives when He is in residence there. Both Michael and I felt Him very strongly there. Michael also met Charles Seage, and we spoke of this upcoming surgery. Upon our return to Portland, we had the last appointment before the surgery was scheduled. The doctor looked at Michael in silence for quite a while. I interrupted the silence by saying, "Are you thinking what I am thinking?"

"Yes," he said, "it looks like that eye socket has somehow aligned itself on its own. I don't think we have to reopen that ear-to-ear incision and peel down and do the big reconstruction I have been planning. I think all we need to do is go back and work more on the nose."

Well, Michael and I were both hugely relieved at this news. And it was obvious that Adi Da Samraj was still Gracing my son at a cellular level that is awesome to witness.

This may sound strange, but one night, as I walked down the corridor to Michael's room, it seemed that Adi Da had not only Blessed my son in all of this, but that His Blessing was spilling out of Michael's room into the adjoining rooms, and in fact into the city, somehow protecting people and stopping for a moment the horrible mortality, pain, and unbelievable suffering that goes on every week in these intensive care units. Some examples:

At one point during Michael's stay in the ICU, I noticed that the completely packed unit—with every bed full when we first got there—was now only at about 40 percent occupancy. Nurses were being sent home because there were not enough critically injured patients on the floor. When I asked them what was going on, they said that patients were getting better faster then expected and that not very many new patients were being admitted with critical injuries.

One Friday night in particular was almost eerie. Friday nights almost always bring tragically injured people into the unit. This particular Friday night—I think it was the third of our stay—there was no one new admitted. No heroic, life-saving efforts. No new business. The nurses said this was <u>extremely</u> rare—and they were delighted. They surfed the web and had coffee instead of providing constant, urgent care.

I also noticed that most of the nurses on that floor brightened up noticeably during our stay there. They were happier, more open, and even giddy at times.

I also remember one night, when Michael was brought back from a major surgery, and most of the nurses came by to give him a hug or a pat on the hand. They praised him for his courage and his strength. Two other patients in adjoining rooms had died during the time of Michael's surgery and so he was a point of light for the nurses, their good news.

This ICU had one room—Room 9—that was equipped for anything that might come up with a critically injured patient. I noticed over the weeks that whenever a patient at the edge of death came into the ICU they went into that room, where many doctors, specialists, and nurses could work all at once to save him or her. I also noticed that the longest anyone was in that room was about four hours, at which point the patient was stabilized and moved to a regular room, or to surgery, or had otherwise died. The nurses told me that that room was reserved for exactly that kind of crisis, and that people were rarely there very long.

This was the room Michael was in the first night of his ordeal. He was in that room for three and a half days.

The enormous Grace of God that Adi Da Samraj has Demonstrated so compassionately in the case of my son stops my mind many moments of every day. I have the rest of this life and beyond to show Adi Da in whatever way I can that I am so thankful for Him and His Work with my son. Michael's recovery is so far beyond what even I, his idealistic father, had hoped for, that I am now simply a witness to a daily miracle.

About four months after the accident, Michael went snowboarding for the first time. He continued to regularly snowboard until they closed the mountain in the spring, at which point he got himself a four-wheeler and ripped up dirt tracks in his recreational time.

His love life is better then ever, and he has returned to work, with no loss of traction there either.

He has also told me that this circumstance of the other car coming out of that back alley at that precise moment, at that speed, and hitting him so directly, could not have been timed more perfectly. He says that a Hollywood writer couldn't script such a thing. He feels that maybe his life had been spinning out of control (which it had), and that this was maybe a serious ass-kicking from the universe.

Looking back, both Chele and I remember Michael acting very strangely the day of the accident. We all work together in the same small office, and Michael was in a very quiet mood on the day before the accident. Both of us had approached him several times to see if everything was okay. He was not himself at all. We were worried.

He had also very uncharacteristically cleaned up his entire workstation at the office—I mean cleaned, organized, and neatly arranged everything around his desk. Now, if you knew Michael at this time, you would know he was a very, very messy guy. Not neat at all. This organization and cleaning was a little shocking, especially with the somber attitude and demeanor he had that day. He must have sensed something about what was to be. That's the only conclusion we can draw.

I also noticed that the crushing injuries he suffered were at what is traditionally known in esoteric literature as the "third eye", or ajna chakra. His throat chakra was directly pierced by the tracheotomy. His navel chakra was completely rearranged from the abdominal surgery. And the blow to his urethra and bladder was exactly in that center of energy. Somehow, it seems he was given a karmic and Spiritual "adjustment" that can't be fathomed.

Michael feels like he was spared and recovered for some reason or purpose that he does not yet understand, but wants to. He is a constant inspiration to be around, and both his sister and myself are buoyed and overjoyed by the time we spend with him. He is humorous, grateful, loving, and humble.

The healing at the heart for our entire family has been awesome as well. I have never been so proud of both of my oldest children and my entire family.

My wife Debbie again overwhelmed me with her instant response to the situation and her sensitive care and love for Michael and Chele and myself.

Michael's sister, at the age of eighteen, showed more strength and poise then anyone I have known my entire life. She dropped her whole life to be Michael's constant advocate at the hospital and I am sure was his primary point of human relationship during this whole event. When he finally woke up, Michael spent about thirty-five minutes hitting his sister in the head with a get well balloon over and over again and smiling at her. They have always loved each other so much, and this was never more apparent.

❖ ❖ ❖

At one point, after Michael became conversational again, I asked him how he was feeling inside—in his emotion, his mind, and his heart.

He said to me, "Dad I haven't been sad, angry, or scared, except for the dreams I told you about. Since I woke up I have been happy only, and I feel a lot of love. I am happier then I was before this happened, by far!"

He asked me again to please thank Adi Da in the strongest way for His Divine Intervention and Help in his life, and he told me he would <u>really</u> like to thank Him, in person, very soon.

Michael Stewart

No Complications

my successful brain surgery

by Bob Kunz
Northern California

My story starts in Adidam Samrajashram, the sacred Hermitage Ashram of Avatar Adi Da Samraj, on the island of Naitauba in Fiji.

It was late in the afternoon of October 31, 2002. I was walking to the kitchen building when suddenly I lost consciousness. When I awoke—feeling <u>very</u> tired—I was told that I had fallen to the ground and lay there shaking for five to six minutes. In other words, I had had a seizure! My Heart-Master, Adi Da Samraj, was informed of my condition.

The next day, I was flown to Suva, the capital city of Fiji, where I had a CAT scan. It did not provide a diagnosis, so I was flown to New Zealand, where I had an MRI. It showed that I had a growth, or lesion, in the back of my head on the right side, about an inch-and-a-half deep and two inches long. The growth had a blood vessel that was leaking slightly. Apparently, the iron from the blood occasionally interacted with neurons, setting off an electrical pattern that shut down the brain.

Needless to say, all of this was confusing and frightening. I felt—perhaps for the first time, at the age of fifty-two—that I could die sooner rather than later. I was told that there was nothing that could be done to cure my condition and that I should take Dilantin, an anti-seizure medication.

I returned to Adidam Samrajashram. I began to take Dilantin but, because of the intense mental and physical side effects, I took as little as possible. Over the next seven months, I had two more seizures, both shorter and less intense than the first. It was obvious that I couldn't stop taking the medication (which I had hoped to do) and that, in fact, I would have to take a larger dose. It was also obvious that I needed to leave Adidam Samrajashram and see if I could get more help for my condition.

In August 2003, I left Adidam Samrajashram and arrived at the Mountain Of Attention Sanctuary, in northern California. Soon after my arrival, I scheduled an appointment with a specialist in epilepsy at the University of California at San Francisco (UCSF). I had another MRI and was told to come back in a week.

Their conclusion was the same as that of the doctors in New Zealand. The lesion was too far inside my brain for surgery and they couldn't do anything for me: I would have to take Dilantin for the rest of my life. But they also encouraged me to seek a second opinion from a neurosurgeon at UCSF.

I did so, seeing a doctor who specialized in the type of lesion I had, a "cavernous blood vessel". After he looked at my MRI, I asked him whether or not brain surgery could cure the problem. He said it was totally doable . . . and asked if I would like to schedule the operation! My jaw dropped—I had been preparing myself for the worst.

Obviously, I felt great that this surgeon was willing to treat me: here was hope! But I also started to realize that he would be opening my skull. Would I end up a vegetable? Could the surgery really cure me? I looked the doctor straight in the eye and asked him how many years he had been performing this operation and how many he performed each year. He said he had been doing them for eight years and that he did fifty to seventy a year. When I heard this, I felt hugely relieved—I hadn't been fully aware of how much anxiety and depression I had been feeling about my condition.

We scheduled the surgery for April 30, about six weeks later.

I began to arrange my life for the surgery. I wrote my Divine Heart-Master, Adi Da Samraj, about the details of the growth in my brain, how it was affecting me and how I was dealing with it. I told him the details of the operation and the scheduled date. And I asked for His Blessing—that the surgery be "completely successful" and that my recovery be "quick and total".

My letter and photograph were presented to Avatar Adi Da two weeks before the operation. That same day, <u>before</u> I knew that my letter had been given to Him, I felt Him combine with my body-mind as an intense force of well-being, so different from my usual sense of self. When I felt Him in this way I became very happy—full of love for Him and the feeling of Him.

The next day, I was told that my letter had been given to Avatar Adi Da. He sent me His Love and Blessings and asked that I be told He was aware of my situation and that He would be informed of the operation a few hours before it occurred.

I felt so Blessed and loved, and so secure, knowing that Beloved Adi Da would have His attention on me during the operation.

I felt so humble and grateful to be His devotee—the Divine Person in human Form had found me and brought me to His Blessing Feet. Tears came to my eyes.

David, a fellow devotee and good friend, said he would be with me before and after the operation and would take care of all communications with my Heart-Master, my friends in the community of devotees, and my family. This was a great relief.

The day before the operation, I went to the hospital to have blood tests, sign papers, and have another MRI. But this time I also had my head shaved, and plastic markers were attached to my

No Complications

scalp so that the MRI could form a 3-D picture of my brain, helping the surgeon to pinpoint the location of the lesion. I looked quite weird!

On Friday, April 30, 2004, David and I woke up early and left for the hospital, arriving and checking in around 6:00 AM. I was taken to a preparation area, changed into a gown, and lay down in a bed. Soon, nurses, an anesthesiologist, and assistant surgeons came around and explained to me exactly what was going to happen.

At around 7:30 AM I was taken into the operating room and they started to prepare my head, securing it so that it couldn't move and cushioning it with foam. Finally, the anesthesiologist gave me a drug. From then on, I don't recall anything.

Avatar Adi Da was informed about the operation a little before it began, and He had His attention on me. I was so glad He was with me. I really felt His Spiritual Presence, there, in the hospital.

The operation lasted five hours—about three less than they thought it would—and it went smoothly. I couldn't help but feel that because Avatar Adi Da had His attention on me, and I had my attention on Him, everything went much better than was expected. I know His Blessing-Regard melted away any complications that might have come up—in myself, in the procedure, in those performing it.

The surgeon's "Recovery Report" was even more positive than he had expected. No numbness. No inability to feel certain parts of the body. No complications.

During the days of my recovery, a report was sent in to Avatar Adi Da about my health and how I was doing. He continued to send me His Love and Blessings. I can feel that my Heart-Master's continued Blessings kept me stable and healthy throughout the whole event. I know in my heart that without Avatar Adi Da's attention on this surgery, there wouldn't have been as positive and strong a recovery as there has been.

❖ ❖ ❖

It has now been six months since the surgery and I am doing well, with continued progress in healing.

I thank my Beloved Divine Guru with all my heart for His Help and Blessing. My life is dedicated to Him. He is my life.

He Saved My Life

the miraculous reversal of a medical crisis

by Tom Williams
Northern California

T he Blessing-Regard of Avatar Adi Da Samraj brought me back from the edge of death.

On the weekend before my medical crisis, I began to experience the kind of pain I usually associate with a gallstone, which I've had in the past. Because I was coordinating a two-day retreat at the Mountain Of Attention Sanctuary, in northern California, I decided to "work through" the pain and go to bed on Monday, hoping to get well before the next weekend, when I had plans to go to Los Angeles.

By Tuesday, however, I was feeling much worse and had a fever. On Wednesday, my fever rose to 102°F and I began to be delirious.

Early Thursday morning, I got up to go to the bathroom, which is about five feet from my bed. But once there, I couldn't stand up and fell backwards onto the floor. A devotee, who was meditating in the Communion Hall below, heard the crash, came up to see what was wrong, found me, and quickly called an ambulance. I was soon in the emergency room of the local hospital, drifting in and out of delirium, with no real sense of how serious my situation was.

JoAnne Sunshine, a friend and fellow devotee, came to the hospital that morning. She relates what happened.

JOANNE: There was a nurse in the room, and I could tell by his quiet intensity that he was very worried. He was extremely attentive, making sure that the IV drops were functioning properly, and he kept checking the monitors, looking for some kind of response to the treatments that Tom was being given to stabilize his condition. Then he tried to fill me in as tactfully as he could, without alarming Tom.

Tom's situation was serious, perhaps even life-threatening. He had developed an infection that had spread throughout his bloodstream. He had been given six liters of IV fluid, which contained five different antibiotics, but the infection had developed to a point where his organs were beginning to shut down. His kidneys weren't functioning and his blood pressure was dangerously low. They were afraid he would soon experience complete organ failure.

The attending doctor came in and began to ask Tom what kind of resuscitation techniques he would allow if his condition further deteriorated. Tom clearly and rationally explained that he would not want to be placed on life-support if there was no chance of recovery. I realized that this situation was <u>much</u> more serious than I had thought when I arrived, and that Avatar Adi Da needed to be notified <u>immediately</u> about Tom's health crisis.

I called Connie, a devotee who is a medical professional, and informed her about Tom's situation so that she could relay the information to Adi Da. Then I began doing the laying on of hands, which (in Adidam) is a healing practice where Avatar Adi Da's Blessing is invoked in the body of a devotee.

But Tom's condition was not improving. And I got the distinct impression from the attending surgeon that he did not expect Tom to live. He had evaluated Tom for surgery—they suspected Tom had an infected gallbladder and wanted to remove it—but decided that Tom wasn't strong enough to withstand an operation. They had tried a potent and somewhat dangerous drug to try to stimulate his blood pressure, but that hadn't worked. The surgeon knew that every medical option had been tried—and Tom wasn't responding. Tom, meanwhile, seemed blissfully unaware of the gravity of his situation.

At some point, I received a call from Connie stating that Avatar Adi Da had been told about Tom.

Within minutes, Tom's blood pressure began to steadily rise—I watched as the numbers on the monitors slowly started to climb for the first time since I had arrived three hours before—and his kidneys started to function.

Soon after this, five other devotees of Adi Da Samraj arrived. We all did the laying on of hands together, surrounding Tom with our devotion and love, invoking Avatar Adi Da's Presence.

The doctors came in to provide to everyone an explanation of what was happening, and they were still communicating very somber expectations. The surgeon explained to us that he had done everything he could, and that we should go home and pray to "Almighty God" for Tom to live through the night. He said he really didn't think Tom would.

Some of us stayed at the hospital and continued to do the Devotional Prayer of Changes. Devotees of Adi Da Samraj worldwide were also informed about Tom's perilous condition and an all-night worldwide prayer vigil was begun. Tom made it through the night. By the morning, his vital signs were stable. Later, the surgeon said, "Indeed, this <u>was</u> a miracle from God. Tom is very fortunate."

Tom has continued to improve and continues to grow in his relationship with Avatar Adi Da—however, with very little memory of these particular events!

I bow down at the Feet of the Ruchira Avatar, Adi Da Samraj, who continuously and miraculously Loves and serves all beings. May this story help inspire those who read it to turn to Him and receive His Blessings.

Tom tells the rest of the story:

TOM: Although I was oblivious to much of what was going on, one thing stands out: in my delirium, I was lost in "mind forms"—in completely random thoughts and images. Then, suddenly, with no effort on my part, I began to experience a current of joy that was somehow underneath and senior to everything else that I was aware of. It was clear to me, even in my delirium, that this was the Presence of Avatar Adi Da. I remember thinking that being overwhelmed by these mind forms must be what the death process is like—and I felt enormously grateful that there was this joyous, fundamental Reality that allowed me to not be identified with my mind.

A week after I came home from the hospital, I received a package in the mail from Adidam Samrajashram, where Avatar Adi Da was residing at that time. In it were dried flowers and two pictures of me, each of which were blurred with water. A note from a fellow devotee informed me that Avatar Adi Da made the watermarks as He anointed my pictures with water during my crisis.

I praise my Heart-Master for His Blessing-Work with me and all beings. I know He saved my life.

The $4000 Wheelchair

*a sudden and unexpected change
in the lives of my father and mother*

by Rick Evans
Northern California

In September 2004, I sent in a request to Avatar Adi Da Love-Ananda Samraj to Bless my eighty-three-year-old father, my eighty-year-old mother (both of whom live in Hamilton, New Zealand, on the North Island), and my fifty-year-old brother, Pete, who lives a mile down the road.

My father had been very weakened by chemotherapy, was arthritic to the point that he could only walk a few yards at a time, and sat rather lifelessly in his chair most of the day. My mother looked after him as well as she could, but had her own health problems. Pete is diagnosed as schizophrenic, and had been recently hospitalized with severe emphysema.

Three weeks later, I received news that Avatar Adi Da had Blessed my parents and my brother on Tuesday, October 19. This occurred during my mother's annual vacation with her relatives in Christchurch, on the South Island. Pete was assisting my father in her absence.

Later in the week, I was surprised and amused to learn from my sister that my father had spent $4000 for a top-of-the-line, motorized wheelchair. This was remarkable, because my mother is extremely frugal (one of her hobbies is searching for supermarket specials), and she is likely to overrule my dad whenever he wants to spend more than a few dollars on any item. I called Pete to get the "inside story", and also to tell him the good news of Avatar Adi Da's Blessing of him and our parents.

Pete expressed gratitude for the Blessing, and said that on Wednesday (the day after the Blessing occurred), dad had phoned the wheelchair company, which is itself surprising, since his arthritis generally makes it impossible for him to dial the phone. He asked the salesperson to come by the house with samples, chose the best model, and wrote the check.

The following day, Pete walked while my father drove his wheelchair to the Returned Serviceman's Association, which is two miles from his house. The next day, they went to the bank, a mile away. And the day after that, Pete said one of his mates called him, amazed to have seen my dad negotiating Hamilton's main street—all by himself, in his new wheelchair.

I was stunned by this development, and felt it was a sign of the Divine Blessings and Influence of Avatar Adi Da. It was <u>so</u> unlike the life that my parents had been living: my father in his chair watching television, and my mother making all the major decisions.

I called my father and, sure enough, he sounded invigorated, and told me that he was feeling restored to the world of the living. Then I spoke to my mother, who complained about the expense, and said that the check had bounced and that she had to call the bank to get payment to go through. She skeptically referred to her husband as "Superman".

As a devotee of Avatar Adi Da, I concluded that something profound had happened. I think the Blessings of Avatar Adi Da are purifying the karmas, or self-created destinies, of my father and mother, helping to relieve them of a pattern that limits their individual lives and their relationship. My father has been struggling all of his life with being controlled, and has made this assertive and radical "statement"—at the age of eighty-three! And I suspect that my mother sees him differently now and maybe respects him more for it.

I praise my Divine Heart-Master, Adi Da Samraj, for His Compassionate Blessings, which help relieve the sufferings of all beings. I bow down to Him in gratitude.

Ward 11

my father's miraculous recovery from pneumonia

by Raewyn Bowmar
Northern California

On December 28, 2003, I received an email from my sister in New Zealand, telling me that my father was "in hospital and quite ill". I called her immediately. She said he had been rushed to the hospital with pneumonia. He was seventy-eight-years old, had suffered several heart attacks, and had a weak liver and other health problems—so I knew that this was a serious and potentially fatal condition.

I was plunged into the chilling reality that my beloved father could die—and very quickly. I had never been threatened with the loss of someone so close to me, and my intense sorrow was the worst emotional pain I had ever felt. I was shocked that there was so much pain, but there was nothing I could do about it except feel it and surrender to my Divine Guru, Avatar Adi Da, continuing with my moment-to-moment devotional practice of turning to Him, even in the midst of my suffering and my father's possible death.

❖ ❖ ❖

Over the next two days I stayed in close contact with my siblings, who kept me updated about my father's condition. On

December 30, my brother told me that the medical staff had asked him if he had called all the members of the family to be at their father's side, because he would not last much longer in his condition. I immediately made travel plans, and left for New Zealand on December 31, fervently hoping that my father wouldn't die before I arrived.

But before I left for New Zealand, I sent in a request to Avatar Adi Da for His Blessings. I knew this was the best thing I could do for my father.

I arrived in Auckland, New Zealand, on January 2, very early in the morning. My brother picked me up at the airport and took me straight to the hospital. He told me that my father's condition had worsened the night before and he had been moved into the intensive care unit (ICU). As soon as I arrived at the hospital I saw my mother, who of course was very upset. Then I went into the ICU. What a shock!

I had never seen anyone so sick, let alone my father. His skin was deathly white. He was hooked up to machines to keep him alive. His face was covered with a special mask that was aggressively forcing oxygen into his lungs. He was obviously very uncomfortable and very distressed. He appeared to recognize me and a tear ran down his cheek. He was trying to speak but wasn't making any sense.

In that moment, the emotion I felt was indescribable—I simply wasn't prepared to see my father so sick and distressed. I went up to him, whispered in his ear how much I loved him, and kissed him on the forehead. I told him that I had written to Adi Da and asked for His Blessing for him. I was crying, and so were my mother and sister. We were all in a kind of shock with the knowledge that we were going to lose him.

The next few days were the most heartbreaking of my life up to that point. To stay close to my father, my family spent most of our waking hours in the hospital. When I wasn't with him, I sat in the waiting room and communed with Adi Da in meditation.

I would also do the Devotional Prayer of Changes. Of course, I prayed for my father's recovery.

During those days, my father was intensely distressed. He kept trying to pull the uncomfortable mask off his face. He kept trying to get out of bed. He kept pleading to go home. Sometimes we could hear him through the mask: "Please, please let me go home for just one day . . . just one day . . . I promise I will come back . . . I want to cooperate . . . just please let me go home."

We knew he was so upset because he was certain he was going to die and wanted to be at home one last time. To see him like this, to hear his desperate pleas, and to <u>not</u> be able to fulfill his wish—he was much too sick to go home, even for one day—was the worst thing of all.

My sister told me that when I was flying to New Zealand from the United States the medical staff kept asking her what time I was arriving: they desperately wanted to keep my father alive until I got there. And there was no improvement in his condition after I arrived. The doctors had tried various antibiotics but none of them were having any effect on the severe pneumonia. My father was getting worse.

On my father's fourth day in the ICU, a doctor got our family together to give us a reality picture. I asked him if there was any chance at all that my father would get through this. He said the chances were "very, very slim"—practically nil, in fact. Even a young person with a lot of physical reserves would struggle to fight such an infection, he said, and would take a year to recover full strength—and my father was fighting the infection with "minus reserves". He told us the machines my father was on could keep him alive indefinitely, and he asked us if we wanted that. We had only to feel my father's terrible distress and pain to help us say that we didn't want that—we knew it wasn't fair to keep him alive in such a dreadful state, no matter how much we loved him and didn't want to lose him. It was a sad and sober moment for us all. The doctor said they would unplug the machines in twenty-four to forty-eight hours and "let nature take its course". We all knew exactly what these haunting words meant, and they struck deep.

On the fifth day in the ICU, my father's condition suddenly and unexpectedly became quite different. He stopped struggling, became very peaceful, and appeared to enter a deep sleep, without intermittent waking. He didn't speak or move. We were happy to see him so peaceful, but we also had the sense that he was letting go of the body and his struggle with it, so it was also emotionally difficult, as we now felt we were facing the imminent reality of his death. The next day, however, he seemed a little more awake, but still relaxed and not struggling. That evening my mother, sister, and I drove home, which was about forty miles from the hospital.

The next morning, my sister and mother went to the hospital a little earlier than I did. I arrived about 11:00 AM. I walked into the waiting room of the ICU—and there were my mother and sister with huge smiles on their faces! They said, "He is going to Ward 11!" (a regular medical ward). I was stunned, and said, "What happened?" They both said, "We don't know." At that very moment, my father was wheeled out in his bed to be taken to Ward 11. No mask. Big smile. Good color. Totally present and clear-minded and speaking coherently. I couldn't believe my eyes. I never expected this, and I found out later that no one on the medical staff did either—they were as mystified as we were.

We followed him down to Ward 11. There he was—and it was unbelievable that he was there. He still hadn't completely recovered, but he was "out of the woods", as they say.

He was in Ward 11 for another two weeks. No one could medically explain why or how he recovered.

During that time, the doctor who admitted him to hospital came in and said with a delighted smile, "Well, I never thought I would see you again."

One of the nurses who was taking care of him said, "Do you realize that your father's recovery is the highlight of my seventeen-year nursing career?" Another time she shook her head in disbelief and said, "You know this is a miracle, don't you?"

We visited him every day and he improved every time we saw him. It was truly amazing. On the first day of my father's recovery in Ward 11, my sister, who had been a nurse, took me aside to tell me that my father would be debilitated when he came out of the hospital and probably would have to go to a nursing home, as it would be too much for our mother to care for him. She said that at his age he would never fully recover from such a serious illness. On the day he came home, he told us with tears in his eyes that when he was being wheeled out of the hospital in a wheelchair, the doctors and nurses lined the corridor in an "Honor Guard" because he had survived something that literally no one thought he could survive.

There is no doubt in my mind or heart that he survived because of Avatar Adi Da's Blessing—there is no other explanation. Adi Da is not an ordinary man—He is alive as Life Itself, as all-pervading Energy and Light, as the Source and Substance of Reality. And His Compassion is beyond imagination—it is a Divine Compassion for all beings, everywhere, because in His Ultimate Identity He <u>Is</u> all beings, everywhere. That He saved my father's life is so obvious to me. I am grateful beyond words for this Gift.

Since his pneumonia, my father is healthier than he has been in many years. But I have noticed another difference in him, at a deeper level. He seems more vulnerable, and relates to life in a more feeling and less superficial way, as if he is living with the knowledge of death. And so are all my family. Adi Da gave us the Gift of more time. Time to feel the depth of the love we have for each other. Time to feel what He calls the "radiant wound of love"—opening your heart to another, even to all others, while also being fully and feelingly aware of their eventual death. This is what Adi Da does, and what He Teaches everyone to do, through His compassionate example and His miraculous Gifts.

The Wound Of Love

from *The Dawn Horse Testament
Of The Ruchira Avatar*
by Adi Da Samraj

Love Does Not Fail For You When You Are Rejected or Betrayed or Apparently Not Loved. Love Fails For You When You Reject, Betray, and Do Not Love. Therefore, If You Listen To Me, and (Also) If You Hear Me, and (Also) If You See Me—Do Not Stand Off From Relationship. Be Vulnerable. Be Wounded, When Necessary—and Endure That Wound (or Hurt). Do Not Punish the other In Love. Communicate To one another, Even Discipline one another—but Do Not Dissociate From one another or Fail To Grant one another The Knowledge Of Love. Realize That each one Wants To Love and To Be Loved By the other In Love. Therefore, Love. Do This Rather Than Make Any Effort To Get Rid Of The Feeling Of Being Rejected. To Feel Rejected Is To Feel The Hurt Of Not Being Loved. Allow That Hurt, but Do Not Let It Become The Feeling Of Lovelessness. Be Vulnerable, and (Thus) Not Insulted. If You Are Merely Hurt, You Will Still Know The Necessity (or The Heart's Requirement) <u>Of</u> Love, and You Will Still Know The Necessity (or The Heart's Requirement) <u>To</u> Love.

The Habit Of Reacting To Apparent Rejection (By others) As If It Were An Insult Always Coincides With (and Only Reveals) The Habit Of Rejecting (or Not Loving) others. Any one whose Habitual Tendency Is To Reject and Not Love others (In The Face Of their Apparent Acts Of Rejection and Un-Love) Will Tend To Reject and Not Love others Even When they Are Only Loving. Narcissus—The

(continued on following page)

Personification Of the ego, the self-Contraction, or The Complex Avoidance Of Relationship—Is Famous For his Rejection Of The Lady, Echo (who Only Loved him). Therefore, If You Listen To Me, and (Also) If You Hear Me, and (Also) If You See Me—Be Vulnerable In Love. If You Remain Vulnerable In Love, You Will Still Feel Love's Wound, but You Will Remain In Love. In This Manner, You Will Always Remain In The human (and, Ultimately, Divine) Sphere Of My Avatarically Self-Transmitted Person Of Love-Bliss.

The Most Direct Way To Know Love In every moment Is To Be Love In every moment. . . .

Those who Love Are Love, and others Inevitably Love them. Those who Seek For Love Are Not themselves Active Love, and So they Do Not Find It. (And, Even If they Are Loved, they Do Not Get The Knowledge Of It.) Only The Lover Is Lovable. Therefore, I Call and "Brighten" Every Heart To Be As True Love Is. And My Every Listening Devotee, My Every Hearing Devotee, and My Every Seeing Devotee Is (By Me) Gifted and (By Means Of My Avatarically Self-Transmitted Divine Spiritual Grace) Enabled To Realize (and, Thus, To Really and Truly Demonstrate) This Radiant (and Radiating) Principle (and Way) Of The Heart—By Means Of True Active (and Freely, Deeply Attracted) Devotional (and Really ego-Transcending) Love Of Me (and With Real, True Trust In Me), The One Who Is (Self-Existing) As Self-Radiant Love-Bliss (or The "Bright") Itself. ∎

"I accept the qualities of all who turn to Me, dissolving those qualities in the Divine Reality."

—Avatar Adi Da Samraj

PART II

Touching the Troubled Heart

Sacred Hair

overcoming my obsessive-compulsive disorder (trichotillomania) by Grace

by Rachel A. LaMell
Chicago

I am ever-grateful to be able to tell my story.

As I write this, I am celebrating a year of sobriety. My "habit" isn't the usual kind of addiction, like alcohol or drugs—but it has taught me a lot about the addictive patterns of the body-mind, and the importance of resorting to my Divine Guru, Avatar Adi Da Samraj.

From a very young age, I had obsessive-compulsive tendencies, things that I would do to feel safe when I was scared—which was quite often! I would touch the same place on a railing, or do something a specific number of times, and so on. Many of these little habits changed over time or were replaced by new habits. At age thirteen, I began to compulsively pluck my eyebrows—not because they were excessively hairy, or for cosmetic reasons, but because I <u>had</u> to keep looking in the mirror and pluck out "the bad hairs".

Pretty soon, I needed to wear makeup to cover up the damage. When I went out in public, I hoped no one would notice my non-existent eyebrows or say anything about them. Unfortunately, they sometimes did, which was quite embarrassing, since I couldn't bring myself to tell anyone that I had done this to myself.

In fact, until a few years ago, I never told anyone about this habit (although my immediate family knew). Until a few years ago, I didn't even know for certain that anyone else did this kind of compulsive hair plucking or that it had a name: Trichotillomania.

Trichotillomania (Trich, for short) is an "impulse-control disorder", with similarities to obsessive-compulsive disorder (OCD). Historically, it was thought to be rare. But, as the condition has become better understood, it is estimated that it may affect 1 to 3 percent of the population. More people are realizing they have it and are seeking help. Even so, there are many people like myself who grow up with this disorder without knowing what it is, and who don't get help until after having had Trich for decades. I want to help change that.

One day, about a year after starting college, for no particular reason, I pulled out a hair from my scalp. And I kept doing it. It felt good, it felt natural, it helped me cope . . . and it became my addiction.

Within a few months, I was wearing a baseball cap everywhere I went, to cover up the bald spots I had created by my "habit". I didn't know anyone else who did this, and I was too embarrassed to tell anyone at school about it. I kept it hidden the best I could (along with my missing eyebrows), and lived in my secret, isolated, tormented world of hair pulling. I pulled mostly when I was alone. But sometimes I did it while other people were around, when they weren't looking.

Over the years, I tried many things to make myself stop, with very little progress or results. I couldn't tell anyone how much I was suffering—I didn't even know how to explain to myself, this insane thing I was doing. I felt the shame and self-hatred build up, layer after layer, as I kept searching—not only for a way to stop pulling, but for better health, for understanding, for Truth, for God.

Sacred Hair

My life became a search to heal, to know <u>something</u> greater than the self-hatred and bondage I constantly suffered.

In 2000, I found something greater—someone, in fact. I became a devotee of Avatar Adi Da Samraj—an Enlightened Being, a person alive as immortal Divine Light and Consciousness—and began to formally practice His Way of Divine Self-Realization, called the Way of Adidam. But I still didn't feel that I could trust other devotees enough to tell them my secret, especially since I was so used to keeping my pulling hidden from everyone. That changed when I met my future intimate partner.

In December 2001, Bruce and I met and it seemed like we were picking up from where we left off—the connection was instantaneous. And I felt completely comfortable telling him about my hair-pulling problem. He knew about addiction, being involved in a twelve-step program himself, and having studied Adi Da's Wisdom on addiction.* And so he encouraged me to learn about and use the twelve steps for my hair pulling, which I did.

I enjoyed some periods of "sobriety", but hair pulling always returned with a vengeance, and I'd have to wear a wig again or otherwise cover up my very short and/or patchy hair. In the spring of 2003, I left my job, didn't have many friends, and rarely wanted to go out in public. My hands, wrists, and arms ached from years of the "repetitive stress" of pulling. I knew I couldn't be happy if my life continued this way.

By the summer of 2003, I had definitely hit bottom, and went to my first twelve-step meeting, which was an open meeting for addicts of any kind.

Around the same time, devotees were informed that they could write a letter to Avatar Adi Da, requesting His Blessing for situations involving themselves, family members, or friends. I immediately wrote—and, as soon as I did, I could feel my situation beginning

---

*Avatar Adi Da describes the separate self (or ego-"I") as an "addict of egoity" (See pp. 113–14). While devotional resort to Avatar Adi Da Himself is the primary practice and most effective Help offered by Him, He also Instructs His devotees to find whatever additional help they need with gross addictions, or other self-destructive patterns, so that they may continue to grow and be more and more available to the devotional and (in due course) Spiritual process in His Company.

to change. The meetings were helping, but when I wrote the letter I could feel my shame being lifted from me.

I asked Adi Da for His Blessing for my continued recovery from Obsessive Compulsive Disorder (OCD), compulsive hair pulling, and for my overall health. I sent the letter the first week in November.

That weekend I was visiting the Adidam ashram in Chicago for a celebration of my Guru's birthday, and I was told that Adi Da had read my letter and given me specific Instructions in response. I couldn't believe it! I was so moved to feel His direct Blessing-Regard and Compassion, His personal Regard of my condition. My suffering was being turned into a Blessing!

Avatar Adi Da sent me His Love and Blessings. He told me that I should intensively practice the devotional Yoga of Ruchira Avatara Bhakti. He said that whenever I had the impulse to pull my hair out, I should think of my hair as His hair—and that I should not pull His hair out!

His humor and Love relieved me of all the years I had suffered this problem alone. To know that I could give this obsession to Him, that I could lay it at His Feet and receive His direct response and Blessing—it was a Grace beyond words.

He Instructed me that in the Way of Adidam, the way to practice with this (or any other addiction) is by turning attention to Him, instead of to the self. With this practice, the addictive pattern becomes purified and, in time, obsolete.

His Instruction also helped me to feelingly connect with Him. Now, whenever I see a photograph of Adi Da, or behold Him over the internet in an occasion of Darshan, I regard His long, beautiful hair, and am heart-attracted by His Freedom and "Brightness".

His Instruction allowed me to practice with all my obsessive-compulsive tendencies, and also to see how I am always an addict if I am not resorting to God. I couldn't have done this without the direct Intervention of the One I recognize as the Divine (my "Higher Power"). I wouldn't have this direct means for self-transcendence. I would have had only a vague sense of something Greater than myself. To know What (and Who) God really is, in Person—to see His beautiful human Form (and hair!)—is the greatest Gift.

The ego-"I" Is an Addict

from *The Basket Of Tolerance**
by Adi Da Samraj

Gross addictions (such as alcohol addiction and drug addiction) are obviously destructive to the individual human being and all of his or her personal and social relations. Therefore, many social and otherwise professional organizations have been developed to help "cure" people of such addictions. However, it is less obvious to mankind in general that the root (or root-cause) of gross addictions is the same root (or root-cause) that is at the base of all ordinary human activity and seeking. That root is egoity (or self-contraction), the primal act (of attention) that appears as the conditional "I" (or the separate and separative self).

The ego-"I" is (inherently and entirely) an addict, a seeker in pursuit of utter self-fulfillment and self-release. No one has ever become an alcoholic or a drug addict who was not first (and already) a self-contracted being (or ego-"I"). And no one has ever been "cured" of (or made responsible for) alcoholism or drug addiction who did not <u>remain</u> a self-contracted being (or ego-"I") and a yet active seeker for utter self-fulfillment and self-release. Therefore, even though to overcome (and to help others to overcome) gross addictions (such as to alcohol or to drugs) is an appropriate and praiseworthy endeavor, the greater Calling of mankind (collectively, and one by one) is to utterly transcend the ego-"I" itself, and all of its patterns of self-contraction (and seeking). And the <u>beginning</u> of the process whereby the ego-"I" is (potentially)

**The Basket Of Tolerance* is an extraordinary masterwork in which Avatar Adi Da Samraj "maps" the entire spectrum of potential religious points of view (as exemplified by all the known religious traditions of human history) through a precisely outlined and extensively annotated bibliography of over 6,000 items (including books, articles, video recordings, and audio recordings).

utterly transcended is the very same (and basically third stage*) discipline whereby the grosser addictions and failures of human life may be overcome. That is to say, human beings must become responsibly able to embrace and maintain a comprehensive practice of self-discipline (and, altogether, an effectively ego-transcending practice of life). And they become thus responsible only by submitting themselves to be guided by an exemplary "culture of expectation and inspiration", wherein they (in a manner that completes the business of the first three stages of life) exercise discriminative intelligence (to the degree of consistently achieving an honest and right self-appraisal, or self-understanding) and, on that basis, consistently exercise the will (via a comprehensive practice of self-discipline, in the general context of an effectively ego-transcending practice of life).

As the members of Alcoholics Anonymous discover (in their course of self-overcoming), the process of truly human growth is (necessarily, and inherently) religious. The ego-"I" is an addict (or a seeker) in everything he or she does. That search is always a lust for objects and effects (whether apparently external or apparently internal). And the search itself is <u>always</u> founded upon "Narcissus"—the basic self-contraction, the alienated, separate, and separative ego-"I". Therefore, to truly understand (and confess) the ego-"I" is to understand (and confess) <u>all</u> seeking (or <u>every</u> kind of addiction). And to truly discipline (and relinquish) any kind of seeking (or addiction) is, necessarily, to relinquish egoity, self-contraction, alienation, separation, separateness, and separativeness. Thus, to truly understand and discipline and transcend seeking (or addiction) and the ego-"I" requires (and more and more becomes) Communion (or re-Union) with (and, Most Ultimately, the Inherently Most Perfect Realization of) the (Self-Evidently Divine) Source-Condition of human (and egoic) existence. ■

*Avatar Adi Da Samraj has described seven stages of human growth and outgrowing, the seventh stage of life being His unique Revelation of Most Perfect Divine Enlightenment. For more about Avatar Adi Da's seven-stage schema, please see *The Knee Of Listening* (Middletown, Calif.: The Dawn Horse Press, 2004).

Avatar Adi Da also told me I should tell my story, so that others will know about this mostly unknown disorder. My reception of this Blessing and Admonition from my Guru has grown in the last year:

Within a few weeks, I was miraculously able to begin telling friends and family about my problem.

I went to a conference held by the Trichotillomania Learning Center, where I met "pullers" from all over the world. (I feel it was only by Adi Da's Grace that I even had the courage to attend the conference.) While there, I was invited to lead a twelve-step discussion. More than fifty people attended the meeting!

I also started a support group for hair pullers and began reaching out and supporting others with this disorder. I am now a resource for people with trichotillomania, and get emails from all over the globe, asking for information and help.

My story is still unfolding. My recovery is definitely a moment-to-moment, day-to-day practice. There are some days it seems easier than others, but I know that my Beloved Guru's Grace is always available to me, when I make myself available to Him— and this has kept me pull-free for over a year. I am grateful for these crazy tendencies I suffer, as they are a constant reminder to turn my attention back to the Divine, instead of keeping it stuck on myself, which only leads to more suffering.

I am so grateful to Beloved Adi Da, for the Blessings He has showered on my life, for the relationship to Him, and for the practice of Adidam that He gives—the practice of allowing myself to be attracted by the One Who Is Happy and Free. I understand how all of us are addicts if we are bound to our own egoic selves. And I know that the "Higher Power" that I call upon is the Divine Heart-Master, Adi Da Samraj—Who my heart recognizes as the Condition of Bliss, Happiness, and Truth, here to Help and Bless all beings.

Relinquish Your Tendencies by Turning to Me

devotion as the True Cure for my chronic anxiety

by David Rosen
Northern California

As a teenager growing up in New York in the 1960s, I was quite moody. Now that is not unusual for a teenager—or a New Yorker! But the <u>predominant</u> mood of my teens and early twenties was anxiety and depression. At times, these negative emotions overwhelmed me, almost to the point of not being able to function. Then, after a few days, they would subside and I would feel great relief—along with anxiety about how long it would be until I started feeling really bad again!

In 1977 I found my Spiritual Master, Avatar Adi Da Samraj. From the first moment I saw Him—in a movie about Him—I knew without doubt that He was my Master, that the incredible attraction and love I felt for Him was the key to Awakening me and all beings from suffering, and that He was the Divine Source of that Awakening, that Freedom, that Spiritual Liberation.

I became His devotee and took on the devotional disciplines that are among the foundation practices of the Way of Adidam. I gave up (without a lot of struggle) a two-pack-a-day smoking habit, and alcohol, and a diet rich in sugar and sweets—and my mood definitely improved. Yet my anxiety continued to surface strongly from time to time, without any obvious cause.

In 1995, Avatar Adi Da Samraj was residing in Adidam Samrajashram, and I was invited to go there on a meditation retreat. While I was incredibly excited about the retreat, getting there turned out to be one of the most anxiety-ridden experiences of my life.

Among my biggest fears is traveling in an airplane, in the dark, over an unlimited expanse of ocean. The flight from California to Fiji was <u>twelve hours</u> of exactly that kind of travel! Then I spent several hours (most of them in the dark) <u>on</u> the ocean, traveling in a medium-sized boat to the island of Naitauba. Both the flight and the boat ride were very rough. At times, I was so overwhelmed by fear and anxiety that I could barely breathe, and I sat for hours quietly sobbing.

At one point during the retreat, I had the opportunity to speak directly to Avatar Adi Da about this ordeal. I was very much hoping for a solution, a consoling word from my Spiritual Master, <u>something</u> to lessen the impact of the anxiety I had felt, and my concern about feeling it again.

After listening to me, Adi Da gazed above my head. I could feel Him beyond . . . beyond the room, beyond the island, beyond the world, beyond the cosmos. After several seconds, in a voice I will never forget, He said, "If you assume the born destiny of presumed separation—then fear is your destiny."

Then He got up and left the room, His Words piercing me to the core.

The Fundamental Illusion of egoity

from a Talk given by Adi Da Samraj
on September 18, 2004

AVATAR ADI DA SAMRAJ: There is nothing about presumed separateness that is not afraid. All presumed separateness is embedded in fear, utterly identical to fear. Therefore, there must be growth in responsibility for the act that is creating the illusion of separateness and, with it, all the accompanying illusions—the illusion of "otherness", the illusion of relatedness, the illusion of "difference". All of your perception at the present time is characterized by these four things, such that you presume that these are fundamental categories of reality. You are you—a separate however-you-describe yourself (body-mind, ego, "I") point of view. There are others here. Relative to any other, you are in relation, rather than identical to them, and there are differences between all things observed. Therefore, it seems that these are the necessary categories of reality. In fact, they are not. They are utterly self-made. They are illusions of your own making.

They have no reality whatsoever, apart from that. And, so, you are afraid. It says in one of the ancient scriptures of India, the *Brihadaranyaka Upanishad,* "Wherever there is an other, fear arises."* Or wherever there is self-contraction, fear arises. In other words, "otherness" is a fundamental illusion of egoity.

If there is the perception of an "other", or the perception (or feeling-sense) that one is separate—if there is the feeling-sense (or observation) of relationship as the condition (or status) of separate self (over against an "other"), if

---

*In Radhakrishnan's translation of this text, the sentence reads: "Assuredly it is from a second that fear arises", where "second" is used in the sense of "other". [*The Principal Upanisads,* edited, with introduction, text, translation, and notes, by S. Radhakrishnan (Atlantic Highlands, N.J.: Humanities Press, 1992), 164.]

there is even the slightest perception of "difference"—fear arises. Fear is inherent in these states. Fear is inherent in self-contraction. Fear is the characteristic mood of egoity. If separateness, "otherness", relatedness, and "difference" were (simply, and really) the case, why would there be fear? It is the case because of the knot, the self-contraction that is making them.

When do you feel pain? When there is a constriction of the natural flows—such as blood and nerve energy, or Energy altogether—then there is pain. When energy is free-flowing, it feels balanced. So—what is this fear? It is a constriction. That constriction exists wherever there is the sense of separateness, "otherness", relatedness, and "difference". Fear is never absent wherever there is that presumption. In That Condition in Which there is no separateness, "otherness", relatedness, or "difference", there is no fear—inherently none.

When (by My Avataric Divine Spiritual Grace) everything that arises is Divinely Self-Recognized, then there is Freedom from the illusion of separateness, "otherness", relatedness, and "difference". In the Demonstration of Self-Abiding Divine Self-Recognition, those characteristics are utterly absent. They are not characteristics of Reality Itself. Therefore, even conditional manifestation is free of this imposition. This is why the Demonstration of Divine Self-Realization is (Most Ultimately) an Outshining of all conditions. Divine Self-Realization is not characterized by dissociation, but by Self-Abiding Divine Self-Recognition. In the egoic state, there is no Divine Self-Recognition. You do not see the way things are. You see them as "things", not as "are". Being is hidden. Its Nature is hidden. The Current of Being is hidden. The Spiritual Force of Existence Itself is limited, even apparently absent.

It is not enough to let the tourniquet slip a little bit. It must be cut, absent—no separateness, no "otherness", no relatedness, no "difference". None. No ego. Reality is inherently egoless. Fear is inherently ego-bound. Yet, the body remains the body even in the State of Realization. If someone who is Awakened is walking through a jungle and tigers leap out from both sides or twelve raptors come from all directions, the sudden reaction will be fear. It is a life-saving reaction. It can be seen to be perfectly intelligent and usable under the circumstances.

It is the consistent, underlying fear coincident with ignorance (or identification with the body-mind) that is transcended in Most Ultimate Awakening. Things as they merely appear remain as such. The Force of Divine Self-Recognition is simply Divine Self-Abiding—until Its Very "Brightness" <u>Outshines</u> conditions. It is not that one becomes merely comfortable being embodied. Rather, embodiment is transcended. Indeed, embodiment is not so. Even in all the appearances of naturalness, it is not so. And, in due course, it is Outshined.

In the meantime, there are the natural appearances, but the Abiding Condition is egoless. There is no root-perception of separateness, "otherness", relatedness, or "difference". There is no obstruction in conscious awareness. There is no tourniquet (or knot) in the Force of Being, the Spiritual (or Love-Bliss-Full) Current of Divine Existence. Most Ultimately, that Current Shines Through and Beyond, such that everything is Vanished in Its Fullness.

Thus, ego-transcendence—and Most Perfect Realization of the egoless Divine Self-Condition—is a kind of death. Not merely natural death—that comes in due course. But Divine Self-Realization is the death you actually fear. And, yet It is not to be feared in the slightest. ■

In 2000 my anxiety worsened—in the form of panic attacks. They usually occurred about an hour after waking up in the morning. A wave of intense anxiety would wash over me and within minutes I would be in a state of total panic—shaking, crying, and completely dysfunctional. After several weeks of this I consulted a doctor, who prescribed an anti-anxiety drug that controlled the panic attacks.

One day, while talking to my mother on the telephone, I told her I was taking this medication.

"Well, dear," she said, "do you know that many, many other people in our family have been treated for depression or anxiety?" My mother started naming these family members and the list went on and on and on!

At least I knew that my anxiety had a genetic component!

In the spring of 2003, my intimate partner Patricia and I were given an extraordinary gift—the opportunity to live for six months in Adidam Samrajashram and serve Avatar Adi Da. This was a transformative time in my relationship to Adi Da. I saw Him almost every day, and He grew me in my capacity to commune with Him and receive His Blessings.

At the end of these extraordinary six months, before leaving Adidam Samrajashram, I wrote my Guru and told Him that one of the great Gifts I had received from Him during this time was a strong trust and faith in Him as my Spiritual Master. I knew that He alone had the capacity to Awaken me to the Realization of Perfect Happiness. I knew that I was completely dependent on His Instruction, Help, and Intervention.

About a year after leaving Adidam Samrajashram, I felt moved to stop taking the anti-anxiety medication. The drug seemed to "lock" the energies of the head and inhibit my emotions—and therefore my heart-communion with Avatar Adi Da. I also began intuiting that something in Adi Da's work with me while I was living in His Hermitage Ashram had moved me into a different phase of my lifelong struggle with anxiety.

At this time, Avatar Adi Da had Graciously offered to Bless His devotees and their families relative to health problems and life-circumstances. It was obvious to me that my anxiety was a core obstruction in my life. I knew that I really, really needed my Master's Help to get through it. I wrote Avatar Adi Da asking for His Blessing.

In my letter, I told Him about the history of my anxiety and depression. I also told Him, in a rather humorous way, that it "ran in the family"—that, as a Jewish child of a Holocaust survivor, I seemed to have inherited a physical and emotional disposition to negative moods.

Soon after I wrote, I received a Communication from Avatar Adi Da.

First, He made a few humorous comments. (Avatar Adi Da often uses humor to put His devotees at ease.) I am a <u>very</u> hairy person. Avatar Adi Da has, on several occasions, joked with me about the fact that He has never seen anybody with as much body hair as me. In this case, He said:

Maybe David's body hair is the cause of his anxiety. He is afraid that his hair is going to take over and cover him completely and he will look something like a gorilla. So he should cut off all his body hair and see if he feels less anxiety.

Then Avatar Adi Da acknowledged that, as a child of a Holocaust survivor, I had in fact inherited a degree of anxiety. Next, He admonished me to get medical assistance in stopping the anti-anxiety drug.

And then, to my surprise, Avatar Adi Da pointed out that even though I had <u>said</u> in my letter that I was devotionally resorting to Him, my concern over my anxiety was evidence that profound devotional turning to Him was <u>not</u> the case:

If there is all this devotion, all this gratitude, all this talk of My Mastery—all these things that are indications of right practice of

Adidam—then why isn't that practice having any effect on his emotional state? These devotional expressions David is making are not fully revealing. They don't indicate the limitations in his actual practice. Real and profound participation in the relationship to Me is what is required.

So he must deal with the matter of his practice for real. He has to function as a devotee of Mine in depth, and seriously, such that it really touches these emotional tendencies of his, which he is holding onto. He is not relinquishing them through turning to Me.

Acting on my Master's Instruction, I got medical help in stopping my anti-anxiety medication. It took about a month to get off the drug.

Anxiety does still arise in me strongly from time to time. But, by my Master's Grace, I have begun to notice something very interesting about how anxiety works.

It usually arises as the result of either a chemical imbalance (which I have to take responsibility for, through dietary change or other means) or a fearful thought.

If I indulge the fear—if I "go with it"—it begins to magnify, and then roots itself in the body. Once this occurs, I am overwhelmed by the fear in a way that has no logic in reality. If, however, before the fear is rooted, I practice the Way of Adidam—if, in response to my Master's Divine attractiveness, I turn my attention, feeling, breath, and body to Him—there is a release or forgetting of the anxiety. This has occurred several times.

In fact, just the other day, I had an extensive dental procedure that, in the past, I have required tranquilizers to get through. This time, I asked <u>not</u> to have the medication and, instead, practiced remembering Avatar Adi Da and turning to Him. To my surprise, I was able to commune with Him through the entire two and a half hours of the procedure. At one point, I even asked the dentist for a mirror so I could watch what she was doing!

I am most grateful to my Master, Adi Da Samraj, for this devotional relationship with Him.

I know that this turning and resort to Him is something that must occur <u>every</u> moment, until there is <u>real</u> transcendence of anxiety. But knowing that He <u>Is</u> Happiness, beyond fear, and that His Help is <u>always</u> there when I truly turn to Him—what an extraordinary Gift!

The Cherry Farm

freeing my son from heroin addiction

by Francine Conrad*

When he was twenty-three, my son came to live with my intimate partner and me. My son and I hadn't lived together since he was ten, when he'd moved to a nearby town to be with his father. I hadn't seen much of him during those years, so I was happy to have the chance to spend time with him and get to know him again. We had a room in a converted garage that all of us felt would work well for him.

He didn't have very much money when he arrived. But with some assistance from my sister he bought a car, and, as an experienced cook, he quickly found a job in a restaurant. Unfortunately, the job turned into a series of jobs—brief jobs. He either quit or got fired, for one reason or another. And each time, a new job seemed harder to find and to keep. He began sleeping during the day and staying out most of the night with his friends. He became less and less communicative. A few months before he arrived, he'd been hit by a car while riding his skateboard, and had been hospitalized for seven days with head injuries. While he appeared to be healed physically, we wondered if he might be having problems staying focused because of the accident.

Then we discovered he was using heroin.

He tried to kick the habit several times on his own, only to start using again after a few days. He was unwilling to enter a rehab program. At some point, he decided to move back to his dad's house, and he started hanging out with the same high school

---

*Name has been changed.

friends who had introduced him to hard drugs in the first place, when he was sixteen. I felt how deeply trapped we all were in this nightmare.

I continued to do the Devotional Prayer of Changes for my son, just as I had many times before. But after several phone conversations with his dad, it was obvious the situation wasn't getting any better.

I realized that I needed to ask my Beloved Divine Guru, Adi Da Samraj, for His direct Blessings. I sent Adi Da my son's photo, with a brief letter describing the situation.

A few days later, I received word that Avatar Adi Da had sent His Love and Blessings to my son. Two weeks later, my son moved to live and work at a cherry farm in Washington State, owned by his father's sister. This change broke the patterns and associations of his drug-using life. It is now a year later—he says he really likes living on the farm, and he has not been using heroin since his move. I feel Avatar Adi Da's Blessing was a truly miraculous and life-saving intervention.

The photo of my son that Adi Da had Blessed was mailed to me, and when I saw it I had an intuition of His immense Divine Sphere of Blessing, far beyond our personal struggles.

About seven months after my son moved to his aunt's farm, I sent Avatar Adi Da a letter of gratitude and an update. Beloved Adi Da sent His Love and Blessings a second time—to my son, myself, my daughter, and my intimate partner—and wanted to know the exact date my son had moved.

Indigo, a fellow devotee, was in the room at the time the update about my son and the photos of him and our family were presented to Avatar Adi Da. She describes the event.

INDIGO: Ruchiradama Quandra Sukhapur read your letter to Beloved Adi Da while He looked at the photos of your son, you, your daughter, and your intimate. He listened intently to the description of how your son was doing, just like your son was a member of His own family. Then He held your photos in one hand, and passed His other hand back and forth over them very slowly and lovingly, like He was feeling all of you. His hand was about an inch above the photos. I felt a welling up of emotion in Adi Da—it wasn't sadness exactly, but a profound compassion, as if He was literally embracing every cell of your body-minds, absorbing them into Himself. To me, it was the same feeling as being hopelessly in love with someone. After He handed the photos back to Ruchiradama Quandra Sukhapur, He sat looking out at the ocean for a moment or two. It was such a profound moment. I couldn't bring myself to look up at His face—that felt too casual—so I kept my head down. It was a great and powerful Blessing for you and your intimates. He is a Miracle.

A Box of Chocolates and a Loaf of Wonderbread

*Divine Instruction and Blessing
in transcending an eating disorder*

by Elaine Gruenke
New York City

I am thirty-two-years-old and I have had an eating disorder—anorexia, bulimia, and compulsive eating—since I was fourteen.

I've been through many years of counseling and therapy since I was first diagnosed. I've also worked with medical doctors, discovering physical factors that contribute to the disorder, like food allergies and celiac disease, and have made healthful changes to my diet. And, for about a year previous to writing this story, I participated in a twelve-step program. The twelve-step program helped me understand that I am an <u>addict</u>—that I have physical (body chemistry), mental, and emotional patterns of food addiction, and that I need to take specific actions to address those patterns.

However, even after years of different kinds of treatments, and the knowledge I have acquired about body chemistry and nutrition, and following the twelve-step program—I <u>still</u> felt confused about, and preoccupied with food and eating, and nothing I had tried seemed to fully address this confusion, or provide me with a clear path through it.

After discussions with other devotees of Adi Da Samraj, I decided to ask Avatar Adi Da for His Blessing-Help regarding my eating disorder. I felt I was suffering to a degree that I couldn't tolerate any longer, and I couldn't remedy my problem with any of the methods I had tried. I felt the only resort I had was to the Person of Avatar Adi Da Samraj. So over a period of several months, I composed a letter to Him, describing my addiction and its medical and therapeutic history, and asking for His Help. I sent the letter, along with photographs of myself and my intimate partner, Joshua.

It came as a complete surprise to me when, some time later, I received an email informing me that my request for Blessing had been presented to Avatar Adi Da. I still felt a degree of guilt and embarrassment about bringing this problem to Him, though I was desperate for His Help. I was very humbled to hear that the request had been presented to Him—and that He had even given me specific Instructions. I sat down on the floor and started to cry with a deep feeling of gratitude and relief.

In His Instruction to me, Avatar Adi Da said that I would have to consider myself an "alcoholic" with food and that, like any addict, I could not be expected to change my behavior on my own. He pointed out that in the twelve-step programs, people have a "buddy" of some sort who they can talk with and be accountable to. He suggested that it might help me to have a person like that—someone within the cooperative culture of His devotees. Avatar Adi Da said that I should be accountable to this person each day, for all the food that I eat. He Indicated that it would not be useful for me to simply be told what to do and expect that I could change my behavior on my own—since I had already had that kind of input in my life and it hadn't worked. But He said that an actual "accountability program" within the culture of His devotees might prove to be useful.

Avatar Adi Da said that I could choose to become "confused" about food, or not—that this was a <u>volitional</u> behavior. This Instruction from Him has helped me to understand that the "confused" feeling I sometimes experience is actually my own choice. Now, when I feel "confused" (and not only about food), I can often observe how, in that moment, I am making a choice to create a "problem"—and that I can just as well choose to <u>not</u> do that.

Avatar Adi Da also remarked that someone should give me a box of Lady Godiva chocolates and a loaf of Wonderbread! Upon reading that, my tears switched to laughter—I couldn't believe how compassionate and humorous He was with me, instead of relating to me only as a person with a "disorder" and a "problem".

Finally, at the end of the transcript of His Communication, I read that Avatar Adi Da Samraj sent His Love and Blessings to me, and to Joshua.

❖ ❖ ❖

Joshua, who was in New York at the time, read the transcript and, following Adi Da's Instruction, bought me a box of fine chocolates. When he got back to northern California (where I was living) he gave me the chocolates—and I had a few agonizing hours of feeling very tempted to eat them. (There are few foods I love more than chocolate.) But I had already found a devotee with whom I had agreed to be accountable for my eating, and after a discussion with her, I had to admit to myself that I was <u>never</u> able to eat just one or two pieces of chocolate without sliding off into a binge.

So I decided <u>not</u> to eat those delicious-looking chocolates, after all. Instead, I gave them to Joshua to eat. I did so with heartbreak and gratitude. Heartbreak, because I couldn't receive this gift of food from Avatar Adi Da and Joshua by simply eating it and enjoying it in an uncomplicated way. Gratitude, because in not eating the chocolates, I stayed emotionally present that evening. Had I eaten the chocolates, I would very likely have felt manic and emotionally removed, and perhaps also triggered a chemical reaction in my body, leading to a binge.

When Joshua finished the chocolates later that week, he gave the box back to me. I still keep it by my Murti as a physical reminder of Adi Da's Blessing.

Since receiving Adi Da's Instruction, I maintain daily accountability with another devotee relative to what I eat. Nevertheless, there are days when I really struggle with my addiction—and sometimes I do indulge. But the discipline of accountability (even on the days when I do indulge) has helped me to see more clearly how I use food, and thoughts about food, as a way of withdrawing from the Divine—in the Person of Avatar Adi Da Samraj—and from the people I love. Becoming more conscious of this "avoidance of relationship" at such a practical level gives me the freedom to choose to stay in relationship instead, even at times when this feels quite difficult.

So Avatar Adi Da's Blessing wasn't a kind of magic, or instantaneous cure. I received His Blessing-Regard and Instruction as Gifts of help and insight, and a call for me to take responsibility for my patterns of thought, feeling, and action.

About two months after receiving Adi Da's Blessings, I felt moved to write Him about how His Instruction was helping me. Instead, I had the remarkable opportunity to speak with Him directly.

This occurred during a period when Avatar Adi Da was giving "Avataric Discourses"—responding to questions from devotees all over the world, connected via telephone and the internet to Adidam Samrajashram in Fiji.

During our conversation, I asked Adi Da about my concern for the fact that thoughts and desires for self-indulgence continued to frequently arise. Shouldn't they be going away, since I was following His Instruction? Was something wrong with me?

In response to my question, Avatar Adi Da said that, just because I was engaging in "right action", I couldn't expect habitual emotional and mental patterns to disappear. He said that my patterning either would or wouldn't continue to arise—whatever was necessary, in my case, for self-transcendence.

He said that the old adage, "through suffering comes wisdom", is only true when one is in relationship to a true Master. Otherwise, suffering only generates more suffering. He said that many people suffer greatly as a result of their own activity, without ever realizing that they are causing their own suffering. So He said that I should continue to follow His Instructions relative to my behavior, and to always remember Him by turning mind, emotion, body, and breath to Him. Adi Da said that the days where it felt more difficult to do this—to turn to Him and stay in relationship rather than indulging my tendencies with food—were days when His purification and Blessing could be more effective.

Avatar Adi Da also told me to practice "faith and patience".

This had special significance for me because it was a reference to a story He has told His devotees many times (and that He had even spoken about earlier that evening) which I very much value:

A female devotee of Shirdi Sai Baba, a Spiritual Master, had repeatedly asked him for a mantra. Shirdi Sai Baba would not give her one. But she kept asking. Finally, Shirdi Sai Baba said that his Master had <u>never</u> given him a mantra. His "technique" for Spiritual Realization was to simply spend time in the Company of his Master—this faith and patience was all that was required.

I was very moved that Avatar Adi Da had referred to this story about Shirdi Sai Baba, as I often listened to a CD of Him telling that story, especially when I was struggling with food. Hearing Avatar Adi Da mention an aspect of the story while He was on the phone with me really helped me feel how His Grace had been available (and always is available) to me in all of my moments of difficulty and struggle.

I have remembered this story many times over the months since speaking with Avatar Adi Da. Adi Da Samraj has never given self-help techniques or methods. Even the Instruction He gave me relative to staying accountable for what I eat is not, in and of itself, a method or technique meant to solve my "problem". Instead, it is a very compassionate and uncomplicated means for bringing to consciousness my own self-caused suffering. Once I understand what I am doing, I have the freedom to choose whether or not to continue doing it. And whole-bodily invocation of the Divine—in the form of turning my body, mind, emotion, and breath to

"Faith and Patience"

from a Talk given by Adi Da Samraj on September 12, 2004

AVATAR ADI DA SAMRAJ: I have often told this story about Shirdi Sai Baba. A woman came to him and took up her lodging near his ashram in one of the many simple hotel-like facilities that were around. She insisted that Shirdi Sai Baba give her a mantra and some specific instructions of a technical kind that she should do as her practice. She pestered him constantly for some kind of instruction along these lines. He finally told her (just to give a general summation, without quoting him specifically): "I am not going to give you any mantra. I never received any. I spent twelve years in the company of my Master. He gave me no mantra. All I did was sit in the room with him, gazing at him. His only instructions were 'nishta and suburi'—faith and patience."

Shirdi Sai Baba practiced twelve years of simply holding himself in his Master's company. In other words, he was simply in Satsang, Darshan, turned to his Master, turned in every sense. There were no instructions to become complicated about or self-conscious about. He was just attending to his Master, serving his Master, turning to his Master, sitting in the room with his Master—with absolute faith in his Master, and patience that, in due course, the Master will do whatever he is going to do whenever he wants to do it. You see? That was Shirdi Sai Baba's instruction to this woman. "Practice this faith and patience. I'm not going to give you a mantra or anything else. You are self-conscious enough as it is! If you want to quiet down and sit in my company, you will benefit (in due course) if you do it truly. And if you do not do it truly, you will show no benefits whatsoever, no matter how many technical exercises you might be given."

The great process of Realization is Given by the Grace of the Master—and that is that. Therefore, the practice is turning to the Master, serving the Master, and attending to the Master. Done rightly and truly, it is an ego-transcending process and it makes you receptive to Me. And I can Do what I Do—My Work—with such a devotee. ■

Avatar Adi Da Samraj—is the necessary foundation upon which this discipline rests, and at the same time, the only "cure" I will ever need.

About a year later, in July 2005, Avatar Adi Da Samraj traveled from Adidam Samrajashram in Fiji to the Mountain Of Attention Sanctuary in northern California. Day after day, I had the Gracious opportunity to be in His physical Presence with many other devotees and guests from all over the world. Each time I was with Him, I experienced the truly Liberating Force of His Presence. A calmness and utter disinclination to any seeking would come over me in His Company, again and again.

Though I am writing this story about what I think and feel Avatar Adi Da is doing to free me from my addictive patterns—the truth is, when I am in His physical Company, I am acutely aware that I really cannot comprehend how His Blessing is working in my body and mind. The Divine is so much greater than anything I can conceptualize. But it <u>is</u> clear to me beyond any doubt that this Gift of relationship to Adi Da Samraj is the most benign, most happy, and, truly, the <u>only</u> means for my Liberation from suffering.

I prostrate at the Feet of the Ruchira Avatar, Adi Da Samraj, the Divine Person alive in our midst, in gratitude for His extraordinary and Compassionate Regard, and His continuous Blessing of all beings, everywhere.

"My Awareness is everywhere.
I Am Meditating every one,
every thing."
—Avatar Adi Da Samraj
August 11, 2004

PART III

Protection from Harm

Thank You, Beloved Adi Da Samraj

the Divine Blessing of a soldier in Iraq and his family

by Algernon E. Crawley Sr., Patricia Battle-Crawley,
and Algernon E. Crawley Jr.
Washington, D.C.

Patricia and Algernon Sr.

Algernon Jr. and wife Hanna

This is the story of the Divine Blessing of Algernon Crawley Sr., a fifty-five-year-old Vietnam veteran, his wife, Patricia Battle-Crawley, age forty-eight, and their son, Algernon Jr., twenty-six, who was with the Fifty-Fifth Signal Company in Iraq.

ALGERNON SR.: It is so wonderful to see your life transformed by the Grace of Avatar Adi Da Samraj.

In 1981, I was reading a newspaper from a health food store in Washington, D.C., and I saw an article about a book titled *Scientific Proof Of The Existence Of God Will Soon Be Announced By The White House!* I purchased the book. Even though the text was challenging and difficult for me to understand, I also knew it was profound, and I kept this book close to me for many years. Little did I know that its words were changing my life.

In the beginning of 1994, something kept saying in my mind, "Get the book!" Even though I heard and felt the statement, I let it go. A month later, I heard, "Get the book! Get the book!" This time I paid attention. Somehow, I knew the voice was telling me to get my copy of *Scientific Proof*.

I started re-reading the book—and this time I began to understand what was being conveyed to me. When I got to the essay titled, "Krishna, Jesus, and the Way of God-Communion", I began to pay very close attention to what was being said. For example:

AVATAR ADI DA SAMRAJ: Human existence is not rightly engaged as an ascetic effort toward separation from the world, the body, and the mind, nor is human existence rightly engaged as an effort toward fulfillment and glorification of the world, the body, and the mind. Human existence is rightly engaged only as ego-transcending Communion with the Living Divine Person, Who Is the Eternal and Self-Existing Acausal Divine Reality in which all beings, worlds, bodies, and states of mind arise, change, disappear, and always inhere, and Who also is Present as the Self-Radiant Energy of every moment of the world, the body, and the mind (if these will only be surrendered and devoted to the One Who Lives them).

When I finished reading this essay, I closed the book and prepared for bed. Suddenly a profound feeling overwhelmed my body—a feeling of utter freedom and release from the human condition. I felt no fear, or any negativity whatsoever. (I've come to understand this feeling as the reception of the Blessing-Transmission of Avatar Adi Da.) At this point I knew I had found my Spiritual Teacher, my Guru. I contacted the Adidam ashram in Washington, D.C., and later attended a retreat with Patricia.

PATRICIA: During the summer of 1995, Algernon Sr. told me about a Spiritual Teacher and a seminar about His Way that was being held in Maryland. I remember telling him to go to this seminar and come home and tell me about it.

When Al got home, he was so full of joy, light, and happiness—I was amazed to see him react this way. He told me about an upcoming weekend retreat and suggested we both attend. And we did. And we continued to go on retreats—because we wanted to learn more about the Divine Heart-Master, Adi Da Samraj. As time passed, we wanted to devote our time—and our lives—to Adi Da. And it's amazing how Adi Da's Divine Love has changed our lives.

In 1998, Al Sr. and I were Blessed to go on pilgrimage to Adidam Samrajashram, in Fiji, and receive His Darshan—the sighting of His Divine (human) Form.

I would like to share the story of the moments before we left Adidam Samrajashram. We had been in the physical Company of our Beloved Guru all night, it was early morning, and Al and I were outside, waiting for a truck to take us across the island to a boat and our departure. We were talking about our experiences of being in such a breathtaking place and of not wanting to leave Avatar Adi Da's Company.

Algernon said, "I wish Avatar Adi Da had given us His Blessing on a personal level."

I said, "Don't move, let's stay right here. You never know what Adi Da might do."

As soon as I said that, a devotee ran up to us and said that Adi Da wanted to see us again, in His house! Algernon took off like a streak of lightning—I didn't know he could move that fast! In all of the excitement, he still remembered to bring the flowers he had set aside that evening to give to Adi Da personally, if the opportunity presented itself. When we went back inside Avatar Adi Da's residence, it was as if the Red Sea had been parted for us to walk through—we walked up and sat down in the front of the room, close to Him. To be that close to Avatar Adi Da—there are no words to describe that experience.

As Adi Da was giving us His Divine Regard, Algernon Sr. and I presented Him with our flowers, from our hearts. Avatar Adi Da appeared touched by our gesture, and He beckoned Algernon Sr. and me to stand before Him. We again presented flowers to Him. This time, He placed His hand over the top of our hands and flowers, in a Blessing motion. Algernon Sr. broke into tears and I stood there in awe, receiving all of His Blessings. To be able to leave all of your worries and concerns, all of your life—everything—to the care of your Divine Master, is wonderful. Thank You, Beloved Da, for Your Love, Your Teaching, and Your Blessing-Presence.

ALGERNON JR.: Ruchira Avatar Adi Da Samraj is exactly what I was looking for—completely satisfying, inherently prior to suffering.

Adi Da's Grace is Perfect. Adi Da <u>as</u> Reality and Truth is immediately apparent when I resort to His Blessing-Gifts, such as His Divine "Source-Texts" and (above all) His Divine bodily (human) Form.

My relationship with and surrender to Avatar Adi Da began with an introduction to Him by my mother and father through His books, Murtis (photographs of Him), and videotapes of His Talks.

His Spiritual Autobiography, *The Knee Of Listening: The Divine Ordeal Of The Avataric Incarnation Of Conscious Light*, was among the first of Avatar Adi Da's "Source-Texts" that I read. Often, when reading *The Knee Of Listening*, I would feel an overwhelming sense of His heart-satisfying Love-Bliss. Avatar Adi Da's Wisdom-Teaching was quenching a thirst I hadn't even known existed in me. In other words, it just felt right! The importance of a relationship with a Guru became increasingly evident to me. In light of such great satisfaction, I felt the urge to write to Avatar Adi Da, and did, thanking Him for the Divine Bliss I was receiving from reading His Scripture and meditating on His Murti.

The Man Of "Radical" Understanding

from *The Knee Of Listening*
by Adi Da Samraj

What appears to the beholder as light, to the hearer as sound, to the shapely actor as life-energy, and to the thinker as thought, is Known directly—on the level of Consciousness Itself—As Love-Bliss.

Then It becomes light, sound, life-energy, and thought.

All such things are only apparent modifications of the Original Reality That <u>Is</u> Love-Bliss.

They are conditionally manifested form.

And conditionally manifested form is that same Love-Bliss.

Love-Bliss is not fundamentally separable from Consciousness.

Love-Bliss Is Consciousness.
Consciousness Itself Is Love-Bliss.
Thus, on the level of activity, there is also no fundamental distinction between thought and form.
There is Only the Love-Bliss That Is Reality Itself—Which is originally, now, Identical to Consciousness Itself.

Conscious Love-Bliss, Unqualified, is the Nature of Reality, Which Is Absolute Existence.
All cosmic powers are communications within this Ultimate Power That Is Existence Itself.
Therefore, the Ultimate Knowledge and Power Is Reality Itself, Which Is Unqualified Existence As Conscious Love-Bliss.
The Unqualified Existence That Is Reality is always already Present, As Love-Bliss.
Love-Bliss is simply Perfect Presence, for Reality is That Which is Unqualifiedly Present.
Present Reality is Conscious As Love-Bliss.
The Man of "Radical" Understanding Only Enjoys Conscious Love-Bliss, at Play.

The Man of "Radical" Understanding does not seek.
The Man of "Radical" Understanding Knows Only Reality.
The Man of "Radical" Understanding Knows Himself Only As Reality.
There Is Only Reality.
His Realization Is Only Reality.
His Knowledge Is Only Consciousness Itself.
He Is Only, Merely Present.
He Is Only Unqualified Existence.
He Is Only Love-Bliss.
He Knows Only Love-Bliss.
There Is Only Love-Bliss.
That Is It—entirely. ■

These joyous experiences occurred around the time my parents were preparing for their pilgrimage to Adidam Samrajashram, to see Avatar Adi Da. Upon their return, I was Blessed and inspired by their remarkable accounts of being in the physical Company of the Divine Guru, Ruchira Avatar Adi Da Samraj.

Eventually, two-and-a-half years after joining the military, on June 2, 2002, I took my formal vow as a devotee in the third congregation of Adidam.* It was a very great feeling and an unforgettable moment. The next day I was on a plane to South Korea.

While I was there, my understanding of the Guru-devotee relationship flourished even more. I was "rolling with the punches" through resort to Avatar Adi Da. I was able to "let go" when necessary, and let life take its course. I was learning that life <u>is</u> as it <u>is</u>, and that I could turn my attention and feeling to Avatar Adi Da under <u>any</u> circumstances.

While in South Korea, I met my beautiful wife—and I grow closer to her every moment through resort to the Person of Love, Adi Da, and His Wisdom on "unqualified relationship".

There is always a time when a family is confronted by life on <u>life's</u> terms. This seemed to be the case when I was faced with a one-year deployment to Iraq. This was a very trying and awkward situation because my tour of duty was being involuntarily extended. One thing for sure, and two things for certain—I was not alone! Avatar Adi Da and my entire family were with me every step of the way.

ALGERNON SR. AND PATRICIA: Al Jr. was to deploy to Iraq in November 2003. We sent letters to our political representatives asking them to intervene—and we also immediately wrote to Avatar Adi Da, requesting His Blessings. He responded with a verbal transmission of His "Love and Blessings" for the Crawley family.

We felt it was by Adi Da's Grace that Al Jr.'s deployment for Iraq was delayed until March 2004. When we realized that nothing else could be done, we surrendered it all to Avatar Adi Da. No matter the outcome, we knew our Divine Guru would Bless Al Jr.

---

*The third congregation of Adidam involves the embrace of the formal Guru-devotee relationship in gratitude to Avatar Adi Da Samraj, and is a means of participation that allows for intensive preparation to embrace the full range of practices as His devotee in the second congregation.

and our family. It was particularly tough for me, Al Sr., to see Al Jr. leave for Iraq, as I am a Vietnam veteran and a Disabled American Veteran (DAV).

ALGERNON JR: Upon my arrival in Iraq—and, quite frankly, in the midst of every aspect of my life—I was aware of Avatar Adi Da's Divine Blessings through recognition of the Blessing-Power of His Divine bodily (human) Form. When I experienced fear, anger, sorrow, or doubt, I would remember to feel Avatar Adi Da's Love for me and allow my heart to break free of the suffering.

In any and every situation, no matter how difficult or challenging, Avatar Adi Da's Love for me and mine for Him was what was <u>most</u> evident and profound. The Divine Gift of Satsang—communion with the Guru—was my key for life. The Guru-devotee relationship provided me with great strength to carry on. It kept my attention in the present, rather than involved with fear about what might happen to me and my family. His constant Blessing of me was the Truth I was living with, moment to moment.

Adi Da's Love and Blessings for me and my family were also Transmitted directly to us via Prasad.

I received Prasad from Avatar Adi Da continuously throughout my tour in Iraq, two dozen times or more. I consider this Prasad—photos of me and my family, flowers, and letters from me to Adi Da, which He received, and then Blessed, anointing them with water—a remarkable treasure, both when I was overseas, and now.

The Blessings from the Prasad were so profound to me that I would carry the Prasad with me. I kept some of the Prasad in my Kevlar helmet and body armor, keeping it as close to my body as possible. When I would go on missions, I would place the rest of the Prasad in a book bag that I carried while on patrol. Having the Prasad with me always helped me feel Adi Da's Love in every moment. I could sense the Prasad protected me—as I was in some very dangerous places, encountering several close calls, which I feel I survived by Adi Da's direct Blessings and Prasad.

I was in Samara during a major offensive, walking the deserted, war-torn streets, advancing toward the front lines with every step. It was at times like that—with intense gun battles and deafening explosions all around me—that I would resort to Avatar Adi Da, feeling His Love and thanking Him for His every Blessing.

I remember one event where I was in the direct line of rocket fire. The round was barely stopped by a ledge of bricks that extended up from the rooftop of a house we had secured and occupied. It exploded no more than twenty feet away but I did not catch a piece of shrapnel, nor did the other soldier I was with.

The Prasad also accompanied me through many towns and villages in Iraq, as I met and talked to local residents and kids. When I met local Iraqis I would try to resort to Avatar Adi Da and remember the Prasad I carried, in the hope that I could be the means for His Divine Blessings to flow to them. I understand that the world may not become a utopia, but Avatar Adi Da's Grace is surely a paradise.

In one instance, Avatar Adi Da used holy water to make His handprint on a letter I wrote to Him, and it was returned to me as Prasad. Once, I touched the handprint left by Avatar Adi Da and felt a charge of energy running up my arm. That charge was a "shock" that definitely put "pep in my step", as "I was as happy as I could be".

His Holy Prasad proved to be an infinite source of Divine Love and Truth. As did His Holy Books.

I studied Avatar Adi Da's Scriptures in my tent while I was in Fallujah. Then I would go sit on the wooden benches in the smoking area and I would feel my body move as I have seen Avatar Adi Da's move in videos or heard about from my parents— in particular, how Avatar Adi Da sits in His seat with His feet on the floor and both hands at His side, as He talks to a gathering of devotees. These feelings would bring a profound sense of Avatar Adi Da into my heart, energizing my satisfaction in Him.

I also had the opportunity to send Avatar Adi Da gifts indigenous to the Middle East, such as a prayer rug and prayer beads. To give a gift to Adi Da is an awesome feeling. It's even greater to hear that He has been pleased by and enjoyed the gift.

Around this time my parents were also sending gifts to Avatar Adi Da in gratitude for His Divine Influence in our lives. They purchased a set of teacups, which Avatar Adi Da used for His evening cup of tea. Indigo, a devotee in Adidam Samrajashram, tells the remarkable story of what happened with one of these cups:

INDIGO: I was called to Avatar Adi Da's house one morning and asked to bring my digital camera. A devotee met me when I arrived and led me over to a white teacup and saucer, which I recognized as one of the Crawley's gifts to Adi Da. She asked me to take a photo of the teacup, especially inside on the bottom.

The devotees who serve at Avatar Adi Da's house had been cleaning His room that morning and were about to take away the teacup He had used the night before. Avatar Adi Da typically has a cup of sage tea at night. The tea is strained, but there is always a little bit of fine sediment left in the bottom. That morning a devotee happened to glance down into the teacup as she was taking it away, and what she saw made her gasp: at the bottom of the cup was a clearly formed, basic shape of a Sanskrit "Da" (द), created by the settling of the sediment.

I checked the cup carefully from all sides, trying to determine if it had been drawn by hand. There was absolutely no chance of that. The way the sediment had settled, and the bit of tea that had started to dry, proved that no hand had touched it. It was a perfectly natural occurrence.

Another devotee, Da-vid Forsythe, was called in to confirm our findings. Da-vid has a scientific background, and Avatar Adi Da had charged him with verifying miraculous occurrences around Him. Da-vid inspected the evidence, and confirmed that the form of the Sanskrit Da had been naturally made.

Teacup with the Sanskrit letter "Da"

ALGERNON JR.: I was very interested in this miracle. I felt that my parents had sent the gift in complete satisfaction with Avatar Adi Da's Divine Incarnation, and with all the love in their hearts.

During this time, I often wrote to Avatar Adi Da, keeping in touch, informing Him of my well-being, and sending current pictures of myself. Often, I thanked Him for His Divine Blessings—for the Gift of remembering Him, the Divine Person, for the Gift of Satsang, the relationship with Him. I would feel greatly Blessed and satisfied when I would hear that Avatar Adi Da received my letter and sent me His Love and Blessings. Via email, I also received photographs of Avatar Adi Da Blessing the letters and photos I'd sent. This was remarkable and encouraging to me—I could see my Beloved Guru . . . and He was holding a picture of me!

The Blessings and Love that Avatar Adi Da bestows upon all, with His every Deed and Word, is exactly the Divine Intervention that brought me home to my family on March 11, 2005.

The Guru-devotee relationship, realized by Avatar Adi Da's Grace, is the primary and most sufficient relationship. With the highest appreciation of Ruchira Avatar Adi Da Samraj, I am writing this as a humbled survivor in the storm of life.

ALGERNON SR., PATRICIA, ALGERNON JR.: We feel the Miracle of Avatar Adi Da's all-pervading Heart-Love. It is wonderful when you realize you have a personal relationship with your Divine Guru. Thank You, Beloved Adi Da Samraj! Thank You, our Beloved Guru Da!

In July 2005, Algernon Crawley Jr. traveled with his wife to the Mountain Of Attention Sanctuary in northern California to directly receive the Darshan of Avatar Adi Da—for the first time in his life. At his first Darshan occasion, Algernon Jr. was embraced by Avatar Adi Da, who hugged him for several minutes. Algeronon Jr. relates the experience:

ALGERNON JR.: Having the devotional sighting of the Divine was basically the answer to my prayers. It was a beautiful time for me, for my wife Hanna, and for my father and mother, who were also there.

But it is very hard to put into words. I didn't have any words at the time, and I don't now. Being in the physical Company of Avatar Adi Da Samraj is remarkable—beyond words. It is one of those things I can't talk a lot about—just the fact of it is what's so amazing.

To be held by Avatar Adi Da, to hug Him and to touch Him—I'm still soaking it in. It's an experience that will always be with me. I was very thankful to be able to see Him. And then to be at the Feet of the God-man and be <u>embraced</u> by Him—that was the epitome of my life.

❖ ❖ ❖

Algernon Jr. and Hanna receiving the Blessing-Regard of Avatar Adi Da Samraj.
The Mountain Of Attention, July 2005

Devotees receiving Avatar Adi Da Samraj's Blessing-Regard as He walks by.
The Mountain Of Attention Sanctuary, 2005

Algernon Sr. and Patricia arrived at the Mountain Of Attention Sanctuary a few days before Algernon Jr. and his wife. They tell their experiences of receiving Avatar Adi Da's Darshan and Blessing-Touch:

ALGERNON SR: For our first Darshan in northern California, Patricia and I were lined up side by side with hundreds of other devotees to receive Avatar Adi Da's Blessing-Regard as He walked along a wide path to His house and looked at every devotee, one by one.

When He saw Patricia and me, He got a big smile on His face and stopped. He turned to me, and I praised Him and thanked Him for Blessing Al Jr. and our family while Al Jr. was in Iraq. And then He Touched my hands with His hand. And when I looked in His eyes, I saw the most beautiful love—the deepest love that I have ever seen in anyone's face. His eyes are like eternal pools of love. Then He turned to Pat.

And then—and I can't explain why I did this, except that Avatar Adi Da helped release any self-consciousness, tension, or nervousness that would have prevented it—I went down on my knees and began to touch and kiss His Feet and His legs and tell

Him how much I love Him. I really wanted Him to feel my thankfulness for what He had done for my family. And as I touched His Feet, He Touched me again, on the side of the face, giving me His love, His all and all. And I broke down and cried.

We stayed five days at the Mountain Of Attention Sanctuary, and received Darshan three or four times a day. On another occasion of Darshan, Avatar Adi Da again looked directly into my eyes, and I could literally <u>feel</u> His Love-Transmission—energy shot down into my body and went all the way to my fingertips and both my hands spread wide open. And I started to cry again—and I couldn't stop. And I lay flat on the ground in devotional surrender, with electricity going through my body, feeling the pure Divine Love of Avatar Adi Da.

He has been so beautiful to our family, and all of us have opened up more and more to His loving Grace.

PATRICIA: When Avatar Adi Da saw us, He gave both of us the most beautiful smile. He Touched Algernon Sr. first, and Al was thanking Him for everything He did for Al Jr. in Iraq and for us as a family.

And when He turned to me, I also started thanking Him for all His Blessings. And He held my hand, and He Touched the side of my face, and my chin—and I felt the world was lifted off my shoulders, that I had no worries because I was with my Beloved Adi Da.

There were other Darshans. And each time I knew I was going to be in His physical Company I could feel my heart going out to Him, and I felt that whatever He needed me to do, I would do for Him. He is the Divine for real, incarnate, here in human Form. He is the Spirit for me. I just love Him.

"See to It They Are in a Safe Place"

Avatar Adi Da Blesses my ill father, my mother, and me

by Debra Hibbs
Boulder, Colorado

Debra with her father Jack

In March 2003, at the age of sixty, my father, Jack, was diagnosed with non-Hodgkins B-cell lymphoma (cancer of the lymphatic system). He had between fifty to sixty tumors throughout his body, and cancer cells in his bone marrow. He had lost one hundred pounds over the past year and he was in a lot of pain.

His doctor said that lymphoma was a very treatable form of cancer and prescribed chemotherapy, with eight rounds scheduled over the next six months. My father responded very well. He had few side effects, and each month the tumors continued to shrink.

In January 2004, a CAT scan showed that most of the cancer was gone, except for some small tumors in his pelvic area and under his arms. But there was also a new, egg-sized tumor on the side of his neck. Concerned, the doctor prescribed a more intensive regimen of chemotherapy: treatments for five consecutive days each month. But after five months, none of the remaining tumors had been reduced in size.

❖ ❖ ❖

In May 2004, I had a dream about my father and Avatar Adi Da Samraj.

First, I should say that throughout my father's ordeal with cancer, I had considered writing Avatar Adi Da to ask for His Blessing for my father, but always found some reason not to. One reason was that the doctor had seemed so sure that he was going to be able to treat the cancer and (before the development of the new tumor) my father was getting better and better. But the biggest reason was my own reluctance to expose the personal details of my life and my family's life so directly to the Ruchira Avatar. I didn't feel that I had a "personal" relationship with Avatar Adi Da, so I wasn't sure that it would be appropriate to tell Him about my personal life and ask Him for such an intimate Blessing of my family.

In the decade that I have been a devotee, I have always served Avatar Adi Da from "behind the scenes": as an accountant in the Sacred Institution of Adidam, in helping prepare His Divine Image-Art for display during the theatrical enactment of *The Mummery Book*,* in making flower arrangements for His environments, and so on. I had never spoken directly to Him, and He had never spoken directly to me, or communicated to me through the recorded and transcribed record of His conversations that are sometimes given to devotees. Somehow—even though I have had the great fortune of seeing Adi Da Samraj many times in Darshan, and I have written many devotional letters to Him—I still didn't feel that I had a "personal" relationship with Him.

In the dream, my father and I were at a large stadium waiting to see Adi Da. In my dream, I realized that I had lost my shoes and was going to have to leave the stadium to search for them. (The Divine Guru has used the metaphor of "putting your shoes in order" to describe the basic preparation that is required to make use of the Spiritual Gifts that He offers.) I turned to my Dad to tell him about my lost shoes, only to find him holding them in the air with a big grin on his face. When I awoke from my dream, I knew that it was time for me to ask Avatar Adi Da to Bless my father.

---

*The Mummery Book is Avatar Adi Da's literary masterwork—a profound parable about the nature of life and Spiritual Realization. *The Mummery Book* is regularly enacted as sacred theatre. For more information, please visit www.mummerybook.org.

It could take years for me to put <u>my</u> shoes in order—but my father didn't have the luxury of time.

I called my parents that day and told them all about Avatar Adi Da's offer to Bless devotees and their family members. I wasn't sure if they would want to participate, and I didn't want to pressure them. They've always been respectful of my relationship with Adi Da, but not necessarily interested in Him or the Way of the Heart.

I explained that I would need digital photos of both of them to accompany the letter of request for Blessing: Avatar Adi Da uses photos as a way to inform Himself psychically about the person He is Blessing and to focus His Blessing-Work. Within a week, they had arranged for a friend to take their photos and emailed them to me. I sent their photos, a gift of flowers, and a letter detailing my father's illness, to Adidam Samrajashram, and requested His Divine Blessing for my father—specifically, that he go into remission and live a long and healthy life with my mother.

At the same time, I also sent my parents a copy of *The Knee Of Listening*, Avatar Adi Da's Spiritual Autobiography. I encouraged my mom to read it and to put it somewhere my father could look at it, if he wanted to. I told her that people often feel a sense of peace or calm when they look at Adi Da's photograph, so my mom propped the book up on a nightstand next to my dad's bed so that he could easily see the large photograph of Adi Da on the cover.

In mid-June, I was told that Avatar Adi Da had received my letter and Blessed my father and mother. He then placed my parents' photos (along with those of myself and my intimate partner, David, which had also been sent to Him) in His Sukra Kendra.

I felt grateful beyond words for His Blessings. I told my parents that we were all in Avatar Adi Da's Sphere of Divine Influence, and that He was working with my dad's cancer.

A few days later, the results of my dad's most recent tests came back—with good news and bad news. There were no longer cancer cells in his bone marrow, but there were new tumors on his chest and liver.

The doctor said the cancer was very aggressive and that stem cell therapy should be considered. But, in the meantime, he prescribed another round of intensive chemotherapy: six hours per day, for four consecutive days each month. At this point, my dad's red and white blood cell counts were very low, as a side effect of chemotherapy, and, as a result, he was very fatigued and sleeping most of the time.

Around this same time, I had another significant dream. For many months, I had been hoping to go on retreat to see Avatar Adi Da at Adidam Samrajashram. In my dream, Adi Da said to me, "Go see your father first, then come see Me." Shortly after having this dream, I called my mom in Florida and arranged a visit in August.

In July, I wrote to Avatar Adi Da right before my father was to begin the next round of chemotherapy, updating Him on my father's condition, and asking Him to Bless my father again—specifically asking "that my father survive this next round of treatments with the most auspicious outcome possible".

This time, I received a Communication directly from Beloved Adi Da saying, "Love and Blessings to Debra, Jack, and Kay".

This completely broke my heart. Not only had Adi Da Samraj, my Divine Guru, sent His Love and Blessings to my parents, but it was also the first time He had ever said my name. I just kept hearing His words running through my head over and over again: "Love and Blessings to Debra, Jack, and Kay." And He called us by our first names, without any seemingly formal use of our surname. How could I have ever believed that I didn't have a personal relationship with my Beloved Guru?

I was also very touched that Avatar Adi Da had Blessed my mother, Kay. The past two years had been very difficult for her.

Her mother died in 2003 and now she was going through this terrible ordeal with her husband, whom she has been with since she was fifteen years old.

❖ ❖ ❖

The same week that Avatar Adi Da Blessed my father again, the doctor discovered that he had become diabetic as a side effect of the steroids he had taken during his treatment. He was sent to an endocrinologist, who prescribed insulin.

A few weeks later, my dad's condition took a miraculous turn for the better. One day at the doctor's office, the nurse noticed that the egg-sized tumor on his neck and the tumors on his chest were no longer visible and couldn't be felt anymore. When she saw this, she exclaimed, "Oh my God!" and ran to get the doctor. The doctor was amazed at the dramatic change in my father's condition. Later, a CAT scan confirmed that the tumors on his neck and chest were completely gone. His red and white blood cell counts were at healthy levels and his blood sugar counts were also in the normal range.

I wrote another letter, thanking Avatar Adi Da and telling Him this good news. This was given to Him in August, and He said, "Love and Blessings to Debra and her father Jack." Again, I was filled with gratitude. When I told my mom about the Blessing, she asked me if she and my dad could write to Avatar Adi Da. Here is the letter:

Dear Adi Da,
    Thank you for your blessings of my husband, Jack.
    My daughter, Debra, is constantly telling us about you. I am now in the process of reading The Knee Of Listening, *and we keep your picture in our bedroom.*
    Thank you again,
    Kay and Jack Hibbs
    Fort Myers, Florida

❖ ❖ ❖

A few days later, on Friday, August 13, Hurricane Charley, a category four hurricane with winds up to 145 miles-per-hour, ripped through Florida. My parents live in Fort Myers, where the hurricane made landfall. They huddled in their closet and packed my father's insulin on ice in case the power went out. My mom mentioned to me that she had moved *The Knee Of Listening* into a drawer to protect it from damage. Fortunately, the most forceful winds of the hurricane were at an angle to their apartment building, rather than hitting it head-on, which would have been far more destructive. The surrounding area lost electricity for many days, but my parents' power was out for just one day.

I flew from my home in California to Florida just a few days after the hurricane had passed and the airports had reopened.

My father was completely bald, but he looked strong and was full of energy.

I brought the Blessed photos that I had received from Adidam Samrajashram (which have a beautiful tie-dyed look from the splashes of holy water on the colored ink) and we hung them on a wall in the apartment.

In early September 2004, Hurricane Frances was heading toward Florida.

Back in California, I received a phone call from Adidam Samrajashram. A devotee informed me that Avatar Adi Da had received the letter of gratitude from my parents. Since they lived in Florida, He wanted me to contact them immediately and then call Fiji to give Him a confirmation that they were safe from the hurricane.

I was completely overwhelmed when I received this message of Avatar Adi Da's concern for my parents' safety. I called my mom, and she assured me that they were safe because the hurricane was not supposed to hit Fort Myers.

The next morning, I received the exact, transcribed Communication that Avatar Adi Da had given about my parents:

Love and Blessings to Debra, Kay, and Jack, and tell them I received a letter from them and that I send My Love and Blessings. And see to it they are in a safe place.

Again, Avatar Adi Da's Compassion and Love deeply moved me. There are no words to describe how I felt.

At present, my father is in remission, and has not received any chemotherapy treatments for over six months. His energy is strong, and my mom says that he's doing great.

I am so grateful to my Beloved Divine Heart-Master for His unceasing Grace and for all of the Gifts that He has given and continues to give to my family, to me, and to the world.

"I Am your Capability—
therefore, your capability
is Unlimited."

—Avatar Adi Da Samraj
December 29, 1995

PART IV

Business and Blessing

The Divine Medicine

Avatar Adi Da Blesses my health clinic

by Louise Darragh-Law
Melbourne

On several occasions, Avatar Adi Da has Graciously given His Divine Blessing to my loved ones. Each time, there has been an apparent synchronicity of events, followed by a benign outcome.

My twenty-four-year-old son had been suffering from a mental illness. At the time I asked Avatar Adi Da to Bless my son, my son didn't know who Adi Da was, or why I had photographs of Him in the house. But the night I asked for the Blessing, my son dreamed of Adi Da.

He came out of his bedroom in the morning carrying a framed photograph of Adi Da, and asked me who the man in the photograph was. He told me about the dream, and said, "Do you think He might help me?" Prior to this point, he had been refusing to take his medication. From that day on, he began to take his medication—and his mental illness began to stabilize.

One of my sisters had major concerns about her health, and was extremely nervous about a particular procedure she required. She was overwhelmed with concern and didn't want to face it, yet she knew that urgent intervention was necessary. She agreed that I could ask Avatar Adi Da for His Blessing.

The morning of the procedure was the same morning that I received word from Avatar Adi Da to give my sister His Love and Blessings. I phoned her to let her know and she went into the procedure with all anxiety removed—chatting lightly throughout, and even making jokes. The procedure was a success and she made the comment that over the next twenty-four hours she was on an inexplicable high of joy and happiness.

Another sister, who lives in New Zealand, had a routine medical procedure, during which the surgeon made a serious error. As a result, she was readmitted to the hospital the same day with acute peritonitis, an infection of the membrane lining the abdominal cavity. The specialists kept her in the hospital for three days, on painkillers and other drugs, unsure how to proceed. Her situation was complicated and critical.

Again, I sent an urgent request for Blessing to Avatar Adi Da. At that point, I was phoning my sister daily. One morning, forgetting the time difference between Australia and New Zealand, I sent her a text message quite early, which woke her up. Later, it was brought to my attention that Avatar Adi Da had given His Love and Blessings to my sister at the exact time that I had sent the text message—so she had been awake while He was giving her His Blessing-Regard.

Over the next week, the complications associated with her condition were greatly reduced and she went on to a full recovery.

Each time I have requested Avatar Adi Da's Blessing for healings, the healing has progressed in a completely benign and favorable manner, and difficulties and complications have dissolved, as if by Grace.

I would also like to describe an instance of Blessing—not of a family member, but of my business—where Beloved Adi Da's Influence was incontrovertibly the case.

I am a healer, not a businesswoman. But healers need business skills if they are to succeed in their healing practice. In August 2003, I was running a small Ayurvedic healing clinic—Ayurvedan Oasis—and I asked Avatar Adi Da to Bless my clinic, that it be aligned to His Teachings on "radical" health and healing.

Avatar Adi Da Teaches that Ultimate Reality is One and Divine: the all-pervading and Transcendental Unity of Conscious Light, the indivisible Substance and Source of existence. He calls the Divine Reality the "Bright".

Be Whole Bodily Healed by Me

from Ruchira Tantra Yoga
by Adi Da Samraj

The cosmic domain is entirely psycho-physical—not merely (or exclusively) psychic (or interior, or egoically subjective), and not merely (or exclusively) physical (or exterior, or apparently objective). If you conform yourself <u>responsively</u> to Me, I "Brighten" <u>all</u> of that.

The human entity is <u>not</u>, in Truth (or in Real Acausal God), a merely separate (or independent) being. Rather, the human entity is a <u>pattern</u>—a psycho-physical pattern in ever-changing interconnectedness with the larger (or collective) pattern of all human entities (and all non-human entities) on Earth. And the human entity, and the Earth-collective altogether, is in ever-changing interconnectedness with the total pattern that is the Earth itself, and the total pattern that is the entire cosmic domain. And the

(continued on following page)

human entity, and the collective of all and (cosmically) All, Always Already Inheres (Non-Separately) in Real (Acausal) God (or That Which Is Always Already the Case). Therefore, there is no Real (or Inherent) separateness (or "difference")—and all apparent separateness (or "difference") is a self-generated (or ego-made, or self-contraction-made) illusion, which (if not directly transcended) always results in egoic (or self-contracted, or separative, and always seeking) activity.

The human entity (and every kind of conditionally manifested entity, or pattern—and even the total cosmic domain itself) is a complex of functions (or functional patterns) which, in the egoic (or self-contracted) mode, either (one by one) contradict (and oppose) or complement (and cooperate with) one another. Indeed, any and every pattern within the cosmic domain (including the human entity) is merely and only a binary (or bi-polar) form. That is to say, every conditional pattern is (in any and every moment) a pattern with only two sides (or options)—either to contract or to radiate. Therefore, in any moment, any pattern (and any pattern, or part, within any pattern) can be either a "closed fist" or an "open hand"—a "no" or a "yes", a "zero" or a "one", a "minus" or a "plus", a negative or a positive, a "pull" (in the contracting sense) or a "push" (in the anti-contracting, or radiating, and entirely open, sense).

The human entity (and even all-and-All) is, as a result of complex self-contraction-reactions over time, a complex (or multi-patterned) ego-pattern (or habit) of "yes's" and "no's", each and every part of which (in any moment) either contradicts or cooperates with each and every other part, in complex relation (or reaction) to all the patterns of change with which "it" (or the presumed, but never exactly and entirely defined, ego-"I", or "center" of experience) is apparently associated. Therefore, every human ego-"I" (and even all and All) must be positively purified and

<u>positively</u> transformed—<u>responsively</u>, and <u>cooperatively</u>. In <u>every</u> <u>moment</u>, the complex human entity, or pattern (or complex of patterns), must be converted from "no" to "<u>yes</u>"—<u>entirely</u> (or in every part), and as an integrated (but not dissociated, or self-contracted, separated, and separative) <u>whole</u>. And, Most Ultimately, even all and All must be converted from "two" to <u>Me</u>—<u>from</u> the apparent broken pattern of many conditionally appearing (and merely temporary) lights and <u>to</u> My Inherently Unbroken Divine Form (Which Is Eternal, and Utterly Non-Dual, and Perfectly Non-Separate, and Indivisibly One).

Therefore, listen to Me and hear Me, and (thus and thereby) understand and transcend your ego-"I" (or separative body-mind-self) in Me. By Means of Me-recognizing and to-Me-responding devotion to Me, surrender, and forget, and transcend <u>all</u> psycho-physical self-contraction, <u>all</u> psycho-physical separateness, and <u>all</u> psycho-physical separativeness. Grow to see Me even every "now" and "where"—and, thus, by turning <u>from</u> the ego-vision of conditional patterns of apparent "difference" and <u>to</u> the Inherently egoless Vision of My Avatarically Self-Revealed Divine (and Perfectly Non-Separate and Non-Dual) Person (and My Avatarically Self-Revealed Divine Pattern of Non-"Difference"), be even whole bodily healed and En-Light-ened (and, Thus and Thereby, Divinely Liberated) by Me. ■

In the year following my request for Avatar Adi Da to Bless my clinic so that it would be aligned to His Wisdom-Teaching on health and healing, I began to experience moments of clarity about the falsity of the subject/object perspective and the truth of Unity. In fact, these experiences began to occur <u>immediately</u> after asking for Adi Da's Blessing.

Ayurveda—a comprehensive system of natural healing from India—was relatively unknown in Australia at the time I started my clinic. My clinic was new and small, and I was managing it single-handedly. It was beginning to expand, however, and I was becoming weary of doing all the healing <u>and</u> business work.

After asking for Avatar Adi Da's Blessing, I took two steps to improve my clinic: I began a small business improvement course, and I booked a study trip to India to improve my Ayurvedic knowledge.

My trip to India was planned to coincide with Avatar Adi Da's sixty-fourth birthday, on November 3, 2003, which would be celebrated in many countries around the world. Along with my request for Blessing, I had requested permission to attend Avatar Adi Da's birthday Celebration in India. This permission had been granted and I had sent a letter of gratitude to Him.

One day, before leaving for India and while working at my clinic's reception desk, I felt suddenly and inexplicably, completely happy and free from all restraints, blocks, pain, and contraction. For a few moments, every limit was lifted from me, and I felt—in mind, emotion, and body—my direct connection to the Divine Reality. The next day, I received an email from Adidam Samrajashram, saying that Adi Da had received my letter of gratitude. The time He got my letter coincided exactly with the Graceful moment of freedom that I had experienced the previous day.

I attended Adi Da's birthday Celebration in Ganeshpuri, a small town near Bombay, and an area of great importance in the sacred history of Adidam.* It was a beautiful evening, with heartfelt chanting and ecstatic devotional dancing. The Celebration, in a village temple, was attended by people from Ganeshpuri and a group of devotees from Australia, Holland, the United States, and India. After the Celebration, other devotees and I sent Avatar Adi Da letters, expressing our love and gratitude and thanking Him for the wonderful opportunity to attend this Celebration.

One night, a week later, while still in India, I woke up shortly after midnight with an overwhelming experience—I felt as if every cell in my body were awakening from a long sleep. I cried my heart out for thirty minutes or more, taking great gasps of air. I felt like I was reawakening ancient memories that I had long forgotten.

---

*Ganeshpuri is home to the ashrams of Bhagavan Nityananda and Swami Muktananda, who served as Avatar Adi Da's Gurus during His process of Divine Re-Awakening.

A few days later, I learned that the time I had this experience was the same moment that Avatar Adi Da had received our letters of gratitude.

However, after my return to Australia from India, I suffered a crisis of confidence: I was overwhelmed at the enormity of my task to successfully practice Ayurveda. I knew that <u>something</u> had changed since I asked for Avatar Adi Da's Blessing and traveled to India. I knew that <u>somehow</u> the experience in India, in which it felt as if ancient memories were awakened, was going to impact my clinic and healing work. I also knew that I no longer wanted to focus on "healing" or "cure" in the ordinary sense of those words. I wanted to learn to trust the Ultimate Source of all, and thereby relinquish the false subject/object presumption. I wanted to embrace my relationship with the Divine Form—manifesting before me as Adi Da Samraj.

The Presumption of Prior Perfection

from *The Eating Gorilla Comes In Peace*
by Adi Da Samraj

The basic principle of health, well-being, and the action of healing is the presumption of prior perfection rather than the motivating problem. One must be established in the presumption that Truth Is Always Already the Case, and, therefore, the Perfect Form of any condition is Already, Priorly, and Presently True of it. It is not that you are a problem, or disease, to be cured (or a hopeless sinner to be saved). Rather, you are Already and Priorly One with the Perfect Condition and the Perfect Form of all conditions that presently pertain, and you are simply operating in order to manifest it (or allow it to manifest itself) in the play of experience. This is the basis of faith and faith healing. This must be true of you if you are to live fully well and in Truth. All cures that occur independent of the "faith presumption" are superficial and deluding. ∎

So I went back to work, nervously and tentatively. I swung from a lack of confidence to surges of strong determination, and feeling that I was on the right track. And, most importantly, I resorted to Avatar Adi Da as the Ultimate Source, the Divine Reality in human Form. I practiced the Way of Adidam, turning mind, emotion, body, and breath to Him, in devotional communion. And the clinic began to change.

Originally, the clinic consisted of consultations and treatments. Then, I decided to start holding workshops. I put my trust in Avatar Adi Da and the all-accomplishing power of His Grace. Twenty-four hours before the first workshop began I only had two bookings. By the next night, I had achieved my goal of nine students. Attendance in further workshops occurred the same way. I began to run Ayurvedic retreats, helped establish and coordinate a two-year Ayurveda training program unique to Australia and, with a friend, introduced a new line of Ayurvedic beauty products into the country.

The effectiveness of Avatar Adi Da's Blessing continues to manifest over time. My clinic's reputation has grown considerably. Travelling new paths into the business world is a challenge for me by tendency, but through resort to Avatar Adi Da, and by His Grace and Blessings, I am able to take the next step. I feel purified of so many delusions and false presumptions about the search for cure—and my clinic and my approach to healing are beginning to reflect this.

The results of Avatar Adi Da's Blessing can be seen at every level of the functioning of my clinic. I asked for my clinic's alignment to His Wisdom-Teaching, but by His Grace, I was given so much more. I was Blessed with the understanding that life is a constant process, an ongoing manifestation of Unity. There is no way of knowing how my clinic will demonstrate the next phase of its unfolding, yet all that is necessary is constant resort to Avatar Adi Da Samraj, allowing myself to be guided by His Divine Attractiveness. He is the Divine Source of all there is.

"I was born so that I could be everyone's Friend, by Helping them to remember to feel and breathe and love and Be the Mystery."

—Avatar Adi Da Samraj

What, Where, When, How, Why, and Who To Remember To Be Happy

PART V

Guidance for Children

A Place to Be with Him

Blessings for my daughter, Adara

by Laura Ballance
Northern California

Laura and Adara

This is a story of an auspicious transformation in life, given by the Grace of the Blessings of the Ruchira Avatar, Adi Da Samraj.

My daughter, Adara, has Cri du Chat Syndrome, a genetic disorder that affects every aspect of her life and development.

In the months before writing this story, I was feeling stressed, exhausted, and depressed from night after night and year after year of interrupted sleep, as I struggled with Adara's patterns of sleep disturbance. I was also dealing with her increasing aggressiveness and self-injurious behaviors, all of which are associated with children with her genetic syndrome.

Right around the time of her eleventh birthday, Adara started sleeping through the night, nearly every night. This began to occur while we were away from home, visiting family, sleeping in unfamiliar beds, and doing things out of Adara's normal routine. If anything, I would have expected her restless nights to be even more disturbed.

The following week, I learned that Adara's father (we are divorced, and Adara lives with me and my current intimate partner) had written to Avatar Adi Da on Adara's birthday, requesting His Blessing for her. When we heard about the Divine Guru's Graceful Regard, and realized that recent changes in Adara's behavior were coincident with Adi Da's Blessings, my intimate partner and I were deeply touched.

Adara continued to sleep through the night for the next two months. And she also spontaneously began to chant in a form similar to the Ruchira Avatara Naama Mantra.* This was especially remarkable because her speech development is so delayed. I never expected her to ever be able to chant anything more than "Da", and had only tried to teach her to chant "Da, Da, Da", as we waved the candle and incense around Adi Da's Murti Form during our simple pujas. So I was delighted to hear her one night in the bathtub, rocking in the bathwater and singing, "Om Sri Adi Da Hridayam", clearly and repeatedly.

Around this time she also started trying to say the "First Great Invocation", one of the simple prayers that Avatar Adi Da has given to His devotees. She actually repeated many of the key words correctly.

One day I found a prism and hung it in a sunny window to cast rainbow light on the walls. When Adara saw the rainbows, she excitedly held up her hands in a gesture of beholding, saying "Da." Then, bringing her hands to her heart, she bowed, prostrating on the floor—the "full-feeling prostration" performed during worship by devotees of Adi Da Samraj.

But the changes in Adara didn't mean that she still wasn't very difficult to care for. One evening, after a particularly difficult time with her, I sat in front of the Murti of Avatar Adi Da and sobbed, begging my Beloved Guru for help. In particular, I prayed for more patience in my caring for Adara.

---

*Adi Da Samraj has given a number of forms of "Ruchira Avatara Naama Mantra", composed of His Names and sacred Titles, as means for His devotees to remember and invoke Him.

A Place to Be with Him

I began to have intense dreams—of being with other devotees, of interacting with Avatar Adi Da, and feeling His Blessings, and of living in a cooperative circumstance with other devotees, in which Adara received lots of attention from others. While I was having these dreams, we were offered the opportunity to move into a cooperative circumstance with other devotees in Marin County, establishing a supportive environment with another family of devotees—in a house in which Avatar Adi Da had actually resided when He had been in northern California! Because of Adara, I hadn't dared imagine such a circumstance, and yet here it was, dropping into our laps, as if gift-wrapped by the Great One.

After some consideration, my intimate partner and I decided to make the move. At first, we had been concerned that the changes would be too challenging for Adara. But as soon as she heard about the possibility, she responded so positively and emphatically that we felt confident this would be a good move for her. It felt so auspicious and Grace-given to even have the opportunity to live in this house where Adi Da had been. Adara excitedly proclaimed that this house is "like a Sanctuary!"

Adara knew what a "Sanctuary" was because, earlier in her life, she had lived a block from one: Da Love-Ananda Mahal in Hawaii. And she had received a life-changing Blessing from Avatar Adi Da Samraj on that very Sanctuary, in April 1996:

It was two months before Adara's third birthday. She was very developmentally delayed, and could not speak or walk. I wondered if there was "anyone home"—she would often look toward me but I never had the sense she was looking "at" me.

It was Easter Sunday.* On Saturday, we had decorated eggs with crayons and dyes as a gift for our Beloved Guru, who was residing there. The next day, we heard that someone had hidden the eggs around the Sanctuary, and that Avatar Adi Da was walking around the grounds on an egg hunt with His family. A small group of us—Adara included—gathered to sit on the lawn at the

---

*Avatar Adi Da has often participated in conventional religious and secular holidays as a means to Work Spiritually with His devotees and those who are otherwise celebrating that occasion on that day.

edge of the Sanctuary, to behold Beloved Adi Da from a respectful distance, as He engaged in this playful activity with His family.

It was a delight to behold Him, even from a distance, and it felt like a great privilege to have Adara there. Usually occasions of Darshan of Adi Da Samraj are formal, and not generally attended by young children. After a while of "hunting" on the grounds, Avatar Adi Da began to walk in our direction—and I felt He was going to interact with Adara in some way.

As Avatar Adi Da approached, Adara was sitting in her father's lap. Adi Da stopped in front of him and said, "Any eggs under this one? Looks like a likely candidate." Then He extended His walking staff to Adara, which she grasped in her little hands. He leaned down and placed His left hand on top of her head. She turned as if to crawl away, and He looked up at a devotee with a knowing gaze, and in His deep voice said, "Exactly." (We all immediately knew that he was referring to the tendency of any person to withdraw from the Divine in what Adi Da calls "the complex habit of the avoidance of relationship".) Adara turned to face Him again, and He bent down and kissed her on the forehead, rubbing her upper back and then her chest over her heart. Then He stood up and regarded her.

Our Beloved Guru then moved off to continue the search for eggs. One of the devotees directly attending Avatar Adi Da came over, gently gathered Adara up in her arms, and rushed off to accompany Avatar Adi Da. She was determined to keep Adara in His Company—and another interaction occurred, where Adi Da noticed that Adara liked to see herself in the mirrored glasses of the adult carrying her. Sometime after that, He went back into His house.

After this interaction of Blessing with Avatar Adi Da, Adara seemed to incarnate in her body. I no longer doubted if there was "anyone home", because she started to relate to me (and others) much more directly. I remember one evening, soon after she received this Blessing, when she was lying on my chest on the sofa—and purposefully leaned her face down to my face and kissed me. She definitely wasn't "avoiding relationship"!

A Place to Be with Him

We've been living in our new circumstance for a couple of months now, and the transition has been so smooth and easeful—the obvious fruit of Avatar Adi Da's Blessing-Regard on Adara's eleventh birthday. And now that we're settled in, Adara is continuing to grow in so many ways, becoming more social and less dependent emotionally on me. I have been getting more rest and have been able to receive the Gift of greater patience that I had prayed for a few months ago.

Instead of constantly struggling with feelings of overwhelm and depression, now I wake up feeling grateful to Avatar Adi Da for giving us a place to be with Him.

In June 2005—a few months after I finished writing the account you just read—Avatar Adi Da traveled from His Hermitage Ashram in Fiji to northern California. And so began a new and miraculous chapter in the story of Adara receiving the Love and Blessings of Avatar Adi Da.

In June, July, and August of 2005, Avatar Adi Da Blessed Adara on five different occasions—with His Touch.

To a devotee, being Touched by Adi Da is an ineffable, precious, wordless communication of His Compassion and Love. It is the Touch of <u>Real</u> God—the Divine Reality Itself. It is the same Blessing that He gives to all when He is anointing photographs with holy water—but now He is anointing with a hug or a kiss, with a hand placed on the top of a head, with the sweetest of smiles, with the profound Regard of His extraordinary eyes that convey His Limitless Feeling.

The first time He Touched Adara was during an occasion of His Darshan at an outdoor shrine at the Mountain Of Attention Sanctuary, shortly after He arrived in the United States, in late June 2005. One by one, each devotee offered a gift of a flower at His Feet—a gift representative of devotional surrender and love. As we brought Adara to Him and she offered her flower, Avatar Adi Da held out His hand for her to put the flower in it, briefly held her flower, and then returned it to her. Then He leaned over and gently put His hand on her head. I was so ecstatic and grateful that He Blessed her like that!

Avatar Adi Da with Adara at the Mountain Of Attention Sanctuary, July 2005.

The next time was at the entrance to Ordeal Bath Lodge, another Holy Site at the Mountain Of Attention Sanctuary. Devotees were chanting, awaiting His Darshan. Avatar Adi Da walked down a wide path from His residence to Ordeal Bath Lodge, and when devotees first saw Him in the distance they began to ecstatically call out His Name—including Adara, who yelled "Da! Da! Da!" over and over, in a high-pitched, musical voice that sounded something like the cry of a bird.

When Avatar Adi Da took His seat to Grant His Darshan, one of the members of the Ruchira Sannyasin Order went to where Adara was sitting and brought her to Him. He started smiling—really big!—and then Touched her head. She was looking right at Him, smiling too. I was overwhelmed with gratitude and love, and so were all the other people who were there.

On another occasion when Avatar Adi Da Touched Adara, He also Touched me, stroking my head very lightly as He walked by. And I was just so in love—so much more in love with Him than

Laura with Adara receiving the Blessing-Touch of Avatar Adi Da Samraj.
The Mountain Of Attention Sanctuary, July 2005

I have ever been in my life. And that day I let my love for Him flow out from me to everyone else—which wasn't hard, because all day people came up to me with tears in their eyes to tell me how moved they were by the sight of Avatar Adi Da Blessing Adara. Everybody felt His Love—a showering of Love on us all, breaking our hearts, overwhelming the ego, opening us up to receive His Blessing.

During this time, Adara has deeply bonded to Avatar Adi Da. Yes, she has always been His devotee, and she has responded to Him and bowed to His Murti, just as we do. But this profound contact with Him has taught her how to be in <u>direct</u> relationship to Avatar Adi Da.

When she woke up on the morning after the first time He Touched her, she said, "I'm a devotee." And she has been saying that very frequently—and very happily.

During the week after the first time He Touched her, I was reading to her from His book for children, *What, Where, When, How, Why, and <u>Who</u> To Remember To Be Happy*. When I got to the part about "feeling the Mystery", Adara got very happy and her eyes filled with tears. I think she was remembering how happy we all were the first time Avatar Adi Da Touched her—how we all cried practically all day. She had become a little concerned about the crying, and we told her that we were crying "happy tears"—wonderful, sweet, totally relaxed, happy tears. And now—along with saying "I'm a devotee"—she says "happy tears". A lot.

The Leela I wrote for this book is titled "A Place to Be with Him". The Leela is still about a place to be with Him. Avatar Adi Da has given Adara a new place to be with Him—the depths of her heart.

Serene Passing

*my seven-year-old daughter's trust
in Avatar Adi Da Samraj*

by Sheriden Vince
Northern California

One evening, in 1996, I watched Avatar Adi Da say goodnight to His youngest daughter. On the surface, the event seemed ordinary. But as they hugged and kissed each other goodnight, the demonstration of loving intimacy was so full, so beautiful, so sweet, and so innocent, that the moment became absolutely extraordinary.

To me, it was a feeling-communication of the paradox and mystery of Avatar Adi Da—the demonstration of the undefended, unconditional love of the Divine Being, incarnate in human Form, for another human being.

I felt what a profound Blessing it was for her—to be the daughter of Adi Da and to be raised under His Divine Guidance and Influence.

And I also was overwhelmed with sorrow—that His Divine Intelligence and Love had been absent from my childhood.

❖ ❖ ❖

About six months later, shortly after my fortieth birthday, my life and my practice of the Way of Adidam changed dramatically when my intimate partner and I discovered, to our mutual surprise, that I was pregnant. It had never been my conscious intention to have a child, and the pregnancy could not have been more unexpected. Almost immediately, I felt this newly conceived being to be a girl.

Although I was in shock at the news, at heart I was certain that this pregnancy was a Gift from my Beloved Divine Guru—a way to intensify and authenticate my practice of the Way of Adidam.

When my daughter was born, Adi Da gave her a beautiful name—Serena Mela. The name, He said, means "serene and joyful celebration of Me (Avatar Adi Da)".

I was overjoyed that her name expressed a disposition of serenity founded in her sacred relationship to Adi Da—a disposition perfectly embodied in the exchange I had witnessed between Adi Da and His daughter, and a disposition that could not have been more opposite to the agitation, upset, and lack of serenity that characterized my childhood.

As I write this, Serena Mela is seven years old. Avatar Adi Da's direct Blessing of her developing life has been continuous. And I know that the real intimacy between her and me, and between her and many others—both human and non-human—is also a Blessing-Grace from Avatar Adi Da, and I am profoundly grateful to Him for this Gift of loving intimacy.

Shortly after Serena Mela turned seven, a camel died that had been living at Fear-No-More Zoo, at the Mountain Of Attention Sanctuary in northern California.*

The camel had been named "Jingle Baba" by Adi Da, and he was the oldest and senior camel among several that live at the zoo. He was a wonderful non-human, with a majestic quality.

---

*For more information about Fear-No-More Zoo and Avatar Adi Da's Wisdom about and work with non-humans, please visit www.fearnomorezoo.org.

Serene Passing

Avatar Adi Da with Jingle Baba at Fear-No-More Zoo

Serena Mela has been visiting the zoo since infancy, and often helps there, as part of her practice of devotional service to Adi Da in the Way of the Heart.

Jingle Baba was her dear friend. His death was her first encounter with permanent loss. And it was amazing to me, and extremely moving, to feel her natural resort to Avatar Adi Da throughout her time of mourning. I was so struck by the relative maturity of understanding displayed in such a young person—an understanding that was so obviously the result of Avatar Adi Da's Wisdom-Teaching to children about death and the Mystery of Existence:

Some day, everybody has what they look like go to sleep and not wake up. Then they forget that part, and they go on to someplace else and look different. Nobody knows what they will look like after what they look like now goes to sleep forever. When you go to sleep at night, you forget what you looked like all day. And when somebody dies, or lets the body go to sleep for the last time, they forget what they looked like when they were alive and awake. It is a Mystery—like going to sleep, or dreaming, or waking up.

—Avatar Adi Da Samraj
*What, Where, When, How, Why, and
<u>Who</u> To Remember To Be Happy*

However, feeling Serena Mela's sorrow for Jingle Baba, I wrote the following letter to Avatar Adi Da, asking for His Blessing of her:

Beloved Lord, Adi Da,
May it please Your Heart to Bless Serena Mela. When Jingle Baba died, she was very sad, as this was the first time she experienced the death of a being she loved. She placed a photograph of You with Jingle Baba next to her bed, and placed a candle in front of the photograph. Even though she expressed for many nights how sad she felt, and asked if Jingle Baba was all right, she knows that You are taking care of Jingle Baba, that he had been a wonderful devotee and non-human friend to You. And when she simply breathed in the Mystery and turned to the photograph of You, she was happy and capable of sleeping without bad dreams about Jingle Baba's death.
It is a miracle of Your Divine Incarnation that a child just seven can be drawn beyond sorrow and loss, through turning to You, in Your bodily (human) Form, as the Mystery. Thank You, Beloved Siddha Guru. I pray that Serena Mela continues to receive the Blessing of Your Grace in her life.
Ever dependent on Your Supreme Grace, and eternally grateful to be Your devotee, I prostrate at Your Feet in love,
Sheriden

A few days later, I received a communication that Avatar Adi Da had received my letter, and that He had sent His Love and Blessings to Serena Mela, to myself, and to her father (Brian).

AVATAR ADI DA SAMRAJ: Love and Blessings to Sheriden, Brian, and to Serena Mela. Tell Serena Mela I was happy that she was able to see how serene and strong Jingle Baba was, showing his profound and natural understanding of the process of death, and his trust. And send her Love and Blessings.

Serena Mela

Ruchiradama Quandra Sukhapur Rani was present while Avatar Adi Da performed His Blessing Puja in response to my request. She sent this communication:

RUCHIRADAMA QUANDRA SUKHAPUR RANI: Avatar Adi Da spent a significantly long time Blessing Brian, Sheriden, and Serena Mela, granting them special Regard, and was visibly touched. I particularly noted Avatar Adi Da's deliberate choice of the word "serene" in His response to Serena Mela's letter.

Later, Serena Mela wrote of her feelings about receiving Avatar Adi Da's Blessings: "I was really happy that Beloved sent me that message! I really felt His love for me and knew that Beloved was taking care of Jingle Baba."

For all His Blessings, I bow down in gratitude at the Feet of my Divine Heart-Master, Adi Da Samraj. He exists purely as Conscious Light, the Heart Itself, and He has made the unfathomable sacrifice, and performed the Compassionate Divine Miracle of being born in human Form, for the sake of all—for Serena Mela, for myself, for her father, for Jingle Baba, for every being, everywhere.

My Self Is in My Heart

my son's remarkable relationship with Avatar Adi Da

by Karl Kaiser
Florida

I discovered Avatar Adi Da Samraj around the time of my son's birth, in 1996.

As I began reading Adi Da's Teaching, I was struck by the incredible breadth and depth of His Wisdom, as well as the "bulletproof" coherence of His vast exposition on practical, philosophical, and Spiritual subjects.

Among His published writings are booklets on raising children in the Way of Adidam called *Love, Wisdom, and Happiness in the First Three Stages of Life*.* They contained many practical suggestions on how to raise mature and Spiritually sensitive children, without succumbing to the temptation of first-time parents to overstimulate a child's self-centered impulses.

Although I was not yet a devotee, I applied many of Adi Da's recommendations in the raising of my son. On several occasions during his infancy, I felt the Presence of Avatar Adi Da's all-pervading Blessing-Grace, and even noticed apparent responses in

---

*For information about Avatar Adi Da's Wisdom-Instruction on conscious childrearing, please visit www.visionofmulund.org.

my son to Adi Da's Spiritual Presence. As my son grew and began asking questions about "God" and "Life", I introduced him more directly to Adi Da, all the while trying not to force my own impressions upon him, but leaving him to develop his own response.

Children Must Be Free and Ecstatic

Excerpts from Adi Da Samraj's Wisdom-Teaching on raising children

Educate everyone—from conception on—to live in freedom, to live in Truth, to Commune with Me and to adapt rightly, stage by stage, to every function of their conditional existence and to the Ultimate, or Non-conditional, Condition That I Am and That I Reveal.

from *Love, Wisdom, and Happiness in the First Three Stages of Life*

Each child must be free and ecstatic at the simple native level of his or her own existence. Children must be awakened to feel that they are associated with an Infinite Power, or Mystery, that sustains them, that gave them birth, that is their Destiny, and that is the Power that moves their entire future if they will associate with It rightly.

from *The Scale of the Very Small*

You must give children the cause and freedom to be ecstatic. Children must understand what ecstasy is, what Happiness is. Parents and teachers should discover the functional dimension to which children are sensitive at every stage of adaptation, and then teach them in those functional terms.

from *The Practice of Ecstasy with Children*

Unfortunately, my son's mother and I separated when he was just three. My former wife didn't like the idea of a Guru, and, on a few occasions when my son seemed to make advances in his own sensitivity to Adi Da, she responded to his enthusiasm with displeasure.

As the years went by, my son adapted by tactfully removing photographs and other signs of his feelings for Adi Da from his home with his mother. This situation, along with the growing willfulness typical of older children, made it increasingly difficult for me to encourage my son to remain open to Adi Da. I especially did not want to impose the issue of his parents' divergent religious perspectives and practices, and thus entwine my son's Spiritual life with the conflicts of his parents.

I became a devotee of Avatar Adi Da in 1999. In 2002, it was decided that my son, then three years old, would have to undergo several intensive medical procedures, including open-heart surgery, to correct an unusual and complicated congenital heart-lung condition. At this time, I brought my son's medical case directly to Avatar Adi Da. He Graced my son and myself with His Blessing-Regard over this difficult year, sending us His Love and Blessings, and even keeping up with the surgeries hour-by-hour.

My son's operations, while lengthy and even more technically difficult than first expected, went very smoothly. During this time, I felt Adi Da's Blessing-Regard descending over the entire hospital campus, and, on one very traumatic occasion, felt the "familiar" feeling of Adi Da's Spiritual Presence directly in my son's heart-region.

After the first operation, my son expressed an intense desire to go to Fiji to see Adi Da, and asked me daily whether I had gotten "permission" for him to go!

Within a few months of the last operation, he was given a clean bill of health by the doctors, who said they were very happy with his progress. None of the many potential complications from his new circulatory system had arisen. And, within six months, my son underwent a growth spurt that moved him from the twenty-fifth to the fiftieth percentile of weight for his age. Moreover, he

My Self Is in My Heart

recovered well from the emotional and visceral fear associated with these many traumatic and invasive physical events.

Before long, my son had moved into his middle childhood, with the surgeries seemingly long-passed.

At this time, on the few occasions we discussed Adi Da, my son seemed rather disinterested. Although he had practiced meditation in the past—"feeling the Mystery", and "breathing out the bad stuff and breathing in the good stuff", as Adi Da recommends to children—he resisted it. I began to lament that he might soon request to terminate any association with Adidam, and so I all but ceased to talk to Him about Beloved Adi Da.

In August 2004, Avatar Adi Da began a period of internet broadcasts from Fiji to devotees all over the world, in which He addressed their questions. This was the first time I had ever seen my Beloved Guru speaking, and the living manifestation of His Humor, Intelligence, Love, and Compassionate Address to devotees drew me to Him even more deeply.

These five- and six-hour broadcasts occurred in the evening in Fiji, but overnight in the eastern United States. So it was that, very early one Sunday morning, while my son slept in the next room, I asked a question directly of Avatar Adi Da by phone.

As soon as I was informed I would be the next person to ask a question, I began to feel Avatar Adi Da's Spiritual Presence in my heart and my home. By the time I began to speak to my Beloved Guru directly, I felt His Spiritual Radiance flowing down like hot honey through the top of my head.

In response to my question about His process of Divine Re-Awakening, Adi Da recounted several incidents in His childhood. As He lovingly described these events, I was drawn to remember events in my own childhood, but this time with a radiant, "love-full" intensity, as if somehow Avatar Adi Da's childhood were the Joy inherent in every childhood itself!

However, what happened later that morning was most astounding of all. After my son awoke, I told him over breakfast about my "phone call" with Avatar Adi Da and His talk about His childhood.

At this, my son immediately launched into countless stories of his own psychic and Spiritual contact with Adi Da, seemingly going back for many years! He recalled with great clarity and enthusiasm detailed encounters with Avatar Adi Da in dreams, while playing with friends, and, especially, during his hospital stay.

While my son enjoys creative story-telling on occasion, the sheer volume, pace, and clarity of these stories far outstripped any typical story-telling session. But my mind was completely blown when he suddenly interrupted these recollections to explain to me very directly that . . .

"My self is in my heart, and inside that is a bright light, and inside that is Adi Da."

Later, I realized that this statement is quite similar to the text of the Narayana Sooktam, an Upanishad from the Vedic tradition of India, adapted by Avatar Adi Da for use by His devotees in their worship of Him:

In The Middle Of The Heart, There Is . . . A White and "Brightest" Star Within . . . In The Right Side Of The Heart . . . The Supreme Self Abides. Only That One Is Real God.

It soon became clear to me that, despite all the emotional turmoil of his parents' divorce, and his conscious suppression of his feelings for Adi Da, my son had been having an intensive, if subliminal, devotional relationship with Adi Da for many years. And this subliminal life had been unearthed and brought to full conscious recollection in one morning, with the Blessing of Adi Da Samraj.

In retrospect, it is remarkable how <u>unremarkable</u> these recollections were for my son. From his point of view, he had always been in a relationship with Adi Da, and there was no shock in finally recalling and talking about it.

Since that morning, my son has felt the need to declare that he will still be a Buddhist "at Mommy's house". But his recollections of Avatar Adi Da persist, including how, during one surgery (probably when his heart had been stopped) Adi Da took him to view his own body from the outside. My son remarked how "strange" his own body appeared to him then, and I sensed from his reaction that this was yet another lesson from Avatar Adi Da: a demonstration of the falsity of identifying with the physical body.

I am joyfully heartbroken that, beneath the realm of psychological stress and suppression that afflicts many children of divorce, and even in the face of my son's own conflicted feelings towards Him, Adi Da has continued to work lovingly and patiently with him, as with any other devotee.

In the summer of 2005, Avatar Adi Da traveled to California, where my son and I had a chance to see Him for the first time in many years. This summer had become an extraordinarily expansive and Grace-Full period, during which Avatar Adi Da granted His Darshan to all devotees, as well as many public guests.

One afternoon, I received a request that my son and I present a gift of a flower to Avatar Adi Da when He granted Darshan. There was no reason given for this request, but I assumed it was due to Avatar Adi Da's Help during my son's medical ordeals.

As we awaited His arrival, I began to recall how frightening and painful the surgeries had been two years before—memories which I realized I had "put behind me"—and I became tearful from the feeling of deep gratitude for Avatar Adi Da's Blessing-Regard at that time.

After Avatar Adi Da had taken His seat, my son and I were brought before Him to offer our flowers. Adi Da Regarded me briefly, and then for a long while, Regarded my son with incredible sweetness and love. There was a rising feeling of love throughout the gathering of people. I began to weep and then my son broke down as well.

Avatar Adi Da gestured for my son to approach, and then embraced Him with the greatest gentleness and affection. My son wept and thanked Him. Adi Da stroked his hair, kissed him, held his face, and put His hand over his heart.

Karl and his son with Avatar Adi Da Samraj.
The Mountain Of Attention, July 2005

My Self Is in My Heart

With every gesture of Adi Da, waves of love swept through the gathering. Loving gestures towards one child seemed to be directly and intimately experienced by every person present, until many among those gathered were weeping. The tangible love felt by all was unmistakably recognizable as "Love"—and yet it felt infinitely more profound and pervasive than the "love" we normally feel.

Eventually, my son sat back down beside me, and we both continued to behold Adi Da. As He continued to Regard my son, I noticed tears on Adi Da's face.

Finally, after a few minutes of this intense tenderness, Avatar Adi Da stood up before all present and became utterly calmed and motionless. It seemed to me that He was Communicating, by way of direct demonstration, His Compassionate Blessing in the face of our loving and our fear of mortality and loss, and His offering to behold and commune with Him, as He Is, in the free and blissful space beyond fear, mortality, and loss.

"Your relationship to Me is the certainty of the Absolute—under all circumstances wherein you are otherwise utterly bereft of certainty."

—Avatar Adi Da Samraj
July 6, 1992

PART VI

Divine Intervention in Death

"You're Already in Ecstasy!"

my father's Blessed death

by Daniel Green
Melbourne

On March 14, 2004, at the age of thirty-five, in an initiation ceremony in Melbourne, Australia, I took a vow of eternal devotion to the Eternal Person—the human, all-pervading, and transcendental Divine Heart-Master, Adi Da Samraj. I became a formally practicing devotee in the Way of Adidam.

On April 24, my father was diagnosed with a brain tumor.

On June 24, at the age of sixty-five, he died.

I didn't make a request for Adi Da's Blessing when my father was initially diagnosed with cancer because I wanted to wait until the exact extent and seriousness of the disease was understood—and because neither my family nor I assumed the disease would be anything but treatable. So my father and my family received Adi Da's Blessing when my father was being moved into a hospice, three weeks before he died. And it was during this time that my Master's Divine Influence—on my father and those around him—was most evident.

I vividly remember the evening in late April, right before my father was diagnosed with cancer. I had been with him at my sister's house. As I was dropping him off at the station for his train, I felt a painful love for him—and an acute sadness. He looked so old and frail, so afflicted by the mortal condition. In my diary that night, I wrote a prayer to Adi Da for my family and for all of humankind—that they find recourse to Real God in the midst of this difficult life. I wrote:

By Your Teaching and Your Grace, I see the mortal organism for what it is, when it is devoid of communion with the deathless Real God. What an empty, horrific fate! I feel this mortality tangibly and nakedly, almost like a sore on the flesh—a dark, sad, heavy, bewildering wound. I almost can't bear to look at it.

The next day my father suffered symptoms that seemed like those of a mild stroke. He was writing a letter to his eldest daughter, Nancy, and found he couldn't control the pen properly. In a slightly confused state, he continued to struggle to address the letter and take it to the post office, all the while getting more frustrated and angry with himself. His main symptoms were a mild disassociation from the entire right side of the body, and a general sense of confusion and disorientation.

The next day, he informed me and my sister about the event and we took him to a radiographer for a CAT scan. The technician there said we should take him straight to the hospital for an immediate evaluation. The doctor at the emergency room examined my father and took an x-ray. He said my father hadn't suffered a stroke—but his symptoms were being caused by a tumor in the left hemisphere of his brain.

That night I engaged the Devotional Prayer of Changes for my father's health, and to be able to serve my father as Adi Da's devotee, to be a means for His Blessings to flow to Dad.

In the middle of the night, I felt Adi Da's all-pervading Spiritual Presence and Energy working deeply in my brain, then moving down the left side of my body, and entering my heart. Then His Force moved over to the right side of my body. I felt that this movement of Adi Da's Spiritual Energy was somehow related to my father's condition, and that I had to surrender deeply to His Spiritual Presence to allow Him to do His Work. The next night, I stayed with my father, and again felt Adi Da's Force, taking hold of my right hand and moving powerfully through the right side of my body.

In early May, my father was admitted to the local hospital, where he underwent numerous tests. Nothing conclusive was found. The following week, he was admitted to the neurosurgery ward of St. Vincent's Hospital, in Melbourne. That Wednesday, the tumor was biopsied. On Friday, we received the results, which showed that my father had a "Grade 4 Glioblastoma multiforme"—a serious, aggressive, fast-growing, and often fatal tumor. It was diagnosed as possibly treatable but most likely incurable. My father was given a few months to live—possibly longer, if radiotherapy was successful—and discharged a week later. Although the prognosis came as a shock, we expected that with the help of radiotherapy he would recover, or at least live a few more years.

My request for Adi Da's Blessings was sent to Him at this time. I asked that whatever my father had to go through, the process would be Spiritually auspicious: that whether he lived or died, he have a positive destiny in Real God. My father said that he did not want any unnecessary prolongation of his life, so I wasn't requesting that kind of miracle.

And it soon became obvious that my father's condition was not as hopeful as we had imagined. He continued to deteriorate, and after suffering a fever and several falls, he was readmitted to the hospital in a delirious state. By the end of May, we had come to terms with the fact that radiotherapy was not going to help, and that my father was going to die. In June, he was moved to Caritas Christi Hospice, in Kew, near Melbourne. I spent the next three weeks living and sleeping in the same room with my father, along with my younger sister Alice and my elder sister Nancy, who had arrived from Scotland.

I was at the Adidam Center in Melbourne when I got the email confirming that Avatar Adi Da had received and responded to my request for His Blessings. I was overcome with a deep sensation of love that filled my heart. He had sent His Love and Blessings, and He had doused with water a photograph of my father, a photograph of myself, and a group photograph of my sister Alice, her son Javari, and my father and me. I wept at this Gift, feeling my Divine Guru's direct and personal Regard, His Love and embrace. I was filled with Him. After writing a letter of gratitude, and performing a puja on Adi Da's Murti Form, I went back to the hospice.

At this stage, my father was bedridden and couldn't even feed himself without help. As the tumor grew, his sense of orientation and coordination were becoming more and more impaired. His speech had become a mere whisper, and he was not able to say more than a few words at a time.

On this day, a friend had brought in a Buddhist nun to visit Dad, and she was waiting in the hall outside my father's room when I arrived. I sat down with Dad and told him that Adi Da had sent His Love and Blessings. I was sitting with my hand on his chest, and, as I said this, a flow of energy moved down from my heart into his. There was a sudden feeling of light and love around us, an ecstatic energy. I knew this was a sign of Adi Da's "Bright" Transmission of His Spiritual Presence. My dad and I sat there, bathed in this happiness, my dad smiling from ear to ear. After a while, he managed to whisper, "I can feel it." I knew exactly what he meant. After this, I left and the nun came in. As she entered the room, she looked at my father and said, "You don't need me. You're already in ecstasy!"

My father was something of a seeker in the "New Age" sense. He spent his life studying the work of various teachers and Spiritual Masters, including Gurdjieff, Meher Baba, and Ramana Maharshi. But despite his eclectic interests, he remained committed to a do-it-yourself approach to Spiritual life, and I was brought up accordingly. By becoming a devotee of Adi Da, I felt I was breaking faith with my father and the do-it-yourself "way" he had shown me. I had broken an unspoken rule, violating my fidelity to my father's authority: I had accepted someone else as my "authority", as being more Spiritually knowledgeable. And although my mind said it was nonsense, on some emotional level I felt a strange and guilty logic: I had become a surrendered devotee of a Guru who definitely was not a "do-it-yourself" teacher, and a month later my father had been diagnosed with terminal cancer!

But my own guilt, and my father's personal decision not to fully submit to the Guru-tradition, which I had come to regard as the true source of Grace and Spiritual Help for humankind, and any possible conflict between us about this matter—all these were purified by an event I consider a direct result of Adi Da's Blessings, His Graceful Influence on our karmic patterns.

On his deathbed, my father decided to become the disciple of a Guru.

He decided that Ramana Maharshi, a Spiritual Master from India who lived and taught in the twentieth century, was his Guru. Avatar Adi Da writes that Ramana Maharshi is "the historical (human) Representative of the Great Tradition Whose Confession (and Process) of Realization was (even in many of Its specific Yogic details) most like (or most sympathetic with) My Own Most Ultimate Process and Confession . . . "* To me, this was a wonderful and blessed development, and appropriate for my father, who throughout his life had studied Ramana Maharshi's books.

At this time, I also received acknowledgement from my dad that he was pleased I had accepted Adi Da as my Spiritual Master—and my dad's acceptance of my relationship with my Guru was a great blessing for me.

We placed a photograph of Ramana Maharshi in my father's room and read to him from Ramana Maharshi's teaching. I also used this opportunity to read to my father from Adi Da's book, *Easy Death: Spiritual Wisdom on the Ultimate Transcending of Death and Everything Else*, which includes Adi Da's detailed and

---

*Adi Da Samraj, *The Knee Of Listening* (Middletown, Calif.: The Dawn Horse Press, 2004), 456.

Compassionate Instructions on the death transition. And I played for my father taped excerpts from a seminar on Adi Da's Teaching on death and dying, which had recently been held in Melbourne.

This period of time was full of Spiritual Energy and Light. Everyone around Dad was affected and uplifted by it. Sitting next to Dad often felt something like being in the Communion Hall at the Adidam ashram in Melbourne, where we meditated on and communed with Avatar Adi Da—the same Energy and "Brightness", the same deep silence and peacefulness. Some excerpts from my diary describe this period:

A day of great Grace today. Spent several hours alone with Dad and the Spirit was very tangible then and throughout the day.

Dad sleeping mostly today. Spent some time with us while he was awake this evening. Very lovely time with him. He's all smiles and love. Very precious being with him like this. So full of profound love and peace.

Sitting with Dad this evening was a deeply healing time for me. Just resting for some time in the "peace that passeth all understanding." Simple, pure, tangible peace. So lovely to be with him like this.

My sisters and I—spending so much time at the hospice—were the people most affected by the energy around Dad. Nancy recalls awakening in the night, and seeing so much light around Dad that she thought it was dawn. Alice recalls waking to see a strange orange cloud swirling above Dad, which suddenly spun back into his body like a vortex. Some of the nurses also remarked on the "good energy" they felt when they came into the room.

Until the last few days of his life, Dad was in remarkably good spirits for someone who was being devoured by cancer—all laughs and smiles when he was awake. The doctor remarked that Dad was suffering from a "happy tumor", and that people often reflect in death the disposition they had shown in life. And although his mental functions were slowly being eclipsed by the brain tumor, he would still make hilarious or penetrating comments, often showing seemingly psychic awareness of what was going on around him. What so easily could have been a disturbed and difficult death became a demonstration of profound acceptance and human love.

Avatar Adi Da writes in "The Heart of Understanding", the prologue to His Spiritual Autobiography, *The Knee Of Listening*: "Death is utterly acceptable to consciousness and life." This was certainly true of my father's death process. Death <u>was</u> acceptable—and it was acceptable because there was also the tangible Influence of (as Adi Da writes) "That Power and Untouchable Gracefulness", which all could feel Present in the room.

There was no recoil from the human reality of the situation, but we all felt sublimed. And, through Dad's surrender, we were able to sense the Reality to which we all must surrender if love and peace are to be the characteristics of our lives.

The Heart of Understanding

from *The Knee Of Listening*
by Adi Da Samraj

Death is utterly acceptable to consciousness and life. There has been endless time of numberless deaths, but neither consciousness nor life has ceased to arise. The felt quality and cycle to death has not modified the fragility of flowers, even the flowers within the human body. Therefore, one's understanding of consciousness and life must be turned to That Utter, Inclusive Truth, That Clarity and Wisdom, That Power and Untouchable Gracefulness, That One and Only Reality, this evidence suggests. One must cease to live in a superficial and divided way, seeking and demanding consciousness and life in the present apparent form, avoiding and resisting what appears to be the end of consciousness and life in death.

(continued on following page)

> The Heart Is <u>Real</u> understanding. The Heart Is <u>Real</u> Consciousness and <u>Real</u> Life. The Heart Is What Merely and Only <u>Is</u>, but Which Is also Appearing In and Behind the conditions of mortal life and its death. Therefore, it is said of old, the One That <u>Is</u> Is neither born nor come to death, not Alive merely as the limitation of form (itself), not Itself (or Entirely) Rendered in what appears, and, yet, It Is the Living One, than Which there Is no lesser other (and no Great or Greater Other), Appearing As all of this Play of changes, but Eternally One, Unchanging, and Free.
>
> There Is Only the Constant Knowledge and Enjoyment of the Heart, moment to moment, through the instant of all conditions of appearance and disappearance. Of This I Am Perfectly Certain. I <u>Am</u> That. ∎

Dad died very peacefully. At the time of his death, Alice was alone with him, and she called me to say that he had stopped breathing.

Certain water phenomena are recognized as a sign of Adi Da's Blessing-Influence, particularly brief showers in sunlight that devotees call "Grace Rain". There was a brief sun-shower as I drove to the hospice. Alice also noticed it, as did her son Javari, who was at school.

When I reached the hospice, Dad had passed.

Adi Da has said that the death transition is a positive event, very much like the birth transition—only the person dying is "birthed" out through the top of the head. And there was a powerful, out-the-top, "ascending" energy in the room where Dad died, which lasted for about three hours.

In the days before Dad's death, I had read to him Adi Da's Instructions about what to do during the first few hours after death, and he had appreciated them. For example: "Release body, emotion, and attention via the upward Energy-flow in the spinal line of the body and toward the crown of the head—until, if Grace will have it, there is emergence from the body-mind via the crown of the head, into the next (or new) dimension of experience."* Now I again read these Instructions to Dad, as Adi Da Instructs his devotees to do with a deceased person in the first few hours after death.

As his body was removed from the hospice room, we put a photograph of Ramana Maharishi on Dad's chest, and I felt an instant psychic response from him, indicating that he was pleased with this.

It is clear to me that Adi Da's Blessing-Work comes from His innate Compassion for all beings. And, in retrospect, I can see how His sublime Influence worked on all of us in different ways, and continues to do so.

For me, there was a tremendous healing of my relationship with my father. During the memorial service, I felt Adi Da's Grace washing me of years of unresolved feelings.

Adi Da's Teachings on the death process resonated with Dad. He wished to have a three-day vigil over his body, as we do for devotees in the Way of Adidam,† and Alice and I helped organize this. His body was kept at a local funeral parlor, and we spent time with the body every day.

On the last day of the vigil, it felt as if Dad had fully and finally departed the body for his new destiny.

The night before the last day of the vigil, I again felt Adi Da's Spiritual Presence and Energy. It was strong, and as I responded, it occurred to me that surrender to Adi Da in the Form of His Spiritual Force—a process of Yoga He describes as "self-surrendering, self-forgetting and self-transcending"—must be somewhat similar to the profound "letting go" of the death process. This surrender went on for a while, until I had a curious vision, more "real" to me than an ordinary dream.

I found myself standing on a platform in a large, underground subway tunnel that was dark and colorless, and hewn out of solid

---

*Adi Da Samraj, *Easy Death* (Middletown, Calif.: The Dawn Horse Press, 2005), 267.

†For more about the three-day vigil and other practices recommended by Avatar Adi Da related to the death process, please see *Easy Death*.

rock. I started walking to the left, towards the dark interior. I sensed something behind me, turned around, and saw a light— a train was coming! I instantly thought of Adi Da. I started to walk towards the light . . . and then I was floating in light . . . and then I saw color, and blue sky ahead. Suddenly, I joyously emerged into the open, and I was so happy, floating like a cloud without weight or form, and clapping my hands.

I knew this vision was somehow related to my father's death transition. And I knew he, too, was happy and in the Light.

As a new devotee, the process of participating in Avatar Adi Da's Blessing Puja was wonderful for me. I was able to enter into an ongoing communication with Him, which strengthened and deepened my devotional relationship with Him in a personal and intimate manner. I wrote to Him six times during my father's transition, and each time there would be a communicated response from Him, giving His Love and Blessings to my father, myself, and my family, and occasionally asking questions about my father's condition.

After my father's death, I received the photographs of my father, myself, and my family that I had sent to Adi Da—they had been splashed with the water that Adi Da uses to direct His Blessing. They were accompanied by the flowers that Adi Da also uses in His Divine Puja of Blessing, and I knew that they had been for a brief time in His Sukra Kendra.

Later, I learned that these photographs were in the Sukra Kendra during the days when we conducted the vigil, when I had the vision, and when I had set up a new Communion Hall in my house.

With deepest gratitude, I surrender my father, in my heart, to the human, all-pervading, and transcendental Real God, to my all-Blessing and all-Loving Divine Heart-Master, Adi Da Love-Ananda Samraj.

A Relatively Good Day

the easy death of my friend

by Antonina Randazzo
Northern California

In July 2004, I was in the Fijian islands, on retreat at the principal Hermitage Ashram of my Divine Guru, Adi Da Samraj.

On July 8, I received an email informing me that a dear friend of mine, Bill (who became a devotee of Avatar Adi Da Samraj in the late 1970s, but had not actively participated in the Way of Adidam for the past two decades) had been diagnosed with a brain tumor, and was scheduled for surgery on July 16. The initial diagnosis was that the tumor was a walnut-sized, fast-growing blastoma, that it had not metastasized, and that with surgery, radiation, and chemotherapy Bill could perhaps live two to five more years.

I replied to the email, requesting Bill's photograph. I received the photo and, on July 16, at the exact time of the surgery, went with another devotee into Temple Adi Da, a potent place of worship where devotees gather daily to invoke their Divine Heart-Master.

We placed the photograph on the altar, bringing Bill directly into Avatar Adi Da's Blessing-Sphere. And, for the next hour, we engaged the Devotional Prayer of Changes. We prayed for a successful surgery and the removal of all the cancer. It was a very powerful experience: each of us deeply felt Avatar Adi Da and His Divine Influence.

The next day I received an email saying the surgeon thought the operation had gone well, with most of the tumor removed. However, he had not been able to take out all the cancer: some of it was too close to a part of the brain that controlled motor skills. Chemotherapy was recommended.

At this stage, Bill had very little mobility on his right side, perhaps due to swelling of the brain, and was very uncomfortable. I continued to pray for him, invoking Avatar Adi Da's Grace for the relief of his suffering.

Three weeks later I got a letter from Bill's wife, Karen. The tumor had completely regrown! The paralysis on Bill's right side had increased and he was distraught and confused. Doctors said further treatment would be of little or no benefit.

Needless to say, this was shocking news. All that could be hoped was that Bill wouldn't suffer much longer and would have a peaceful death. So I prepared a request for Blessing from Avatar Adi Da.

The synchronicity of this event and my own life of self-transcending practice of the Way of Adidam was striking to me. During my recent retreat, I had spent many hours in Adi Da's physical Company, as He discoursed to devotees on the mortal condition and the importance of using life for the purpose of Spiritual growth, for Awakening beyond suffering into the deathless Love-Bliss-Full Condition of His Divine Person. I felt an urgency about intensifying my practice of Ruchira Avatara Bhakti Yoga and this helped me serve Bill, Karen, and their family during this intense time of heartbreak and need.

Every morning, soon after arising, Avatar Adi Da receives the day's requests for His Blessing. Early on the morning of August 15, I was in Suva (a town on one of the larger islands of Fiji), engaged in an urgent back-and-forth, via email, with devotees in Adidam Samrajashram, to prepare a Blessing request for Bill for that day.

A Relatively Good Day

Adi Da always receives a photograph of the individual He is being asked to Bless, along with photographs of the immediate family. I had sent a photograph of Bill and of Karen, thinking that was sufficient. But I was asked if there were any children . . . and could I get their photos . . . and their names . . . and their ages . . . and find out where they lived. I was on the computer for hours, chatting with friends in California, where Bill lived, compiling this information. Finally, everything was sent in.

A few hours later, we received word that Avatar Adi Da Samraj had Blessed the entire family and put the photos in His Sukra Kendra.

During the day, I felt an absolute certainty that Bill and his family would feel Adi Da's Graceful Influence and Help. I also personally felt Adi Da's Divine Regard, since my photo was sent in as well, as the devotee who had brought this situation to His attention. I knew my friends were in Adi Da's hands. I felt grateful and at rest.

Later in the day, Adi Da granted another occasion of formal Instruction to devotees, which I was watching on the internet. At the start of this gathering, I received an email, saying that Bill had passed away. It was 7:15 PM Fiji time, on Sunday, August 15. I wept when I heard the news of his passing, and felt what a Miraculous Grace had occurred: I could not believe how quickly Bill had been relieved of his suffering after receiving Adi Da's Regard. I notified devotees at Adidam Samrajashram immediately.

During the gathering, a devotee told Adi Da the news of Bill's death. In response, He said to the dozens of devotees in the room:

A man asked Me for Blessing this morning and I was just told he died a couple of hours ago. He was alive this morning. He got My message of Love and Blessings and My Regard. I put his picture in My Sukra Kendra, and now he is gone. He didn't do several more weeks or months of intense suffering. He had a relatively good day.

The next day, I talked to Karen. She said that when Adi Da's Love and Blessings had been communicated to Bill, he was able to let go and die in peace. She said that she had been reading an excerpt from one of Adi Da's books [see below], and he had died peacefully while listening to the Divine Word of Adi Da Samraj.

My Sphere of Love-Bliss

from a Talk given by Adi Da Samraj on March 28, 1994

AVATAR ADI DA SAMRAJ: What you would have in Communion with Me is a cool, watery, full moonlit night, cooled of stress, and desire, and consolation, Awake to "Brightness".

On that basis, visions of clarity and peace.

And then moving beyond them to My Love-Bliss Itself, without the slightest image, without the slightest object, without the slightest fear, without any "other"—not even yourself an "other".

No "other".
No separation.
No visions.
No objects.

Only Self-Existing Being, Self-Radiant without limitation.

No separate self.
No objects.
No cosmos.
No seeking.

Utterly rested.
Fearless.
Unmoved.

No place.
No going and coming.

No conversation.
No society.
No world.
No sex organs.
No thing.
But Fullness Itself, not objective.

Only God.
Only "Brightness".
No "difference".
No relatedness.
Only Happiness.
No un-Happiness.
No threat.

This is What there is to be Realized, not the mayhem you are manufacturing in your fear and seeking, in your contraction into separateness.

Devote your life to this Peace Beyond "difference", this Divinity, this Communion with Me.

Everything else is just something to be noticed, just a discipline to be applied, more intense practice of this devotion to Me.

All the superficial matter temporary, not important.

Be still.
Be washed.

Be mindless.
Bodiless.
Sublime.
God Only.

"We are Home now, Lord."

That is it.
Do not leave. ∎

LOVE AND BLESSINGS

❖ ❖ ❖

A three-day vigil was held over Bill's body, just as it is for actively participating devotees of Adi Da. I received an email about the vigil from a friend who was in attendance. I thought the story of the vigil honored Adi Da's Blessing-Work with Bill and sent it to Adidam Samrajashram. The next day, it was read to Adi Da, and He again sent His Love and Blessings to the family. This is the story, in the words of the person who sent it to me:

Thanks to the devotees of Adi Da Samraj and to the Grace and Personal Regard of the Spiritual Master. I don't have to be puzzled any longer about Adi Da's phrase, "Sudden Grace".

Instead of all of us looking back upon this week as one of the saddest of times, Bill's wife and kids are already beginning to view it as one of the truly happy and graceful moments of their lives.

And Bill got a prayer of twenty-three years answered—he got to be with his Spiritual Master.

He was dying and in pain. That was the bald truth of it, but the Blessings of the Spiritual Master turned the whole thing around for the whole family.

Bill's wife and daughters have, of course, been doing some crying (I've been a little teary myself when they are not looking), but they are crying happy tears. And the tears are often times followed by laughter.

After Bill died, we allowed his body to lie still for about three hours before we moved him to the room that we had prepared with a little shrine, his favorite picture of Adi Da, some candles, incense, and some flowers. When we carried Bill into the room and placed him in the casket, I was arranging his clothes and placing his hands the way they were when he took his last breath—one resting on his tummy and the other by his side. That is when I finally paused to look at him, and it was amazing . . . he had the most blissful look on his face.

I elected to take the first shift on our vigil, which began at 3:00 AM. The following day, I learned that while I was reading Adi Da's Wisdom-Teaching on death out loud to Bill, to help with his transition, Adi Da was speaking about Bill to His devotees. I couldn't help saying to myself, "Yes, Yes!"

That afternoon I said to Bill's wife, "Can I make a suggestion?" She said, "Yes." And I said, "From now on, don't ever use that vigil room for anything but a meditation room." She replied, "I was just thinking the very same thing." We both feel that room has been Blessed.

I'll close with a quote from "My Sphere of Love-Bliss"—the passage that was being read aloud to Bill as he died. It is an exchange between a devotee and Adi Da:

"We are Home now, Lord," said the devotee.
"That is it," said Adi Da. "Do not leave."

In August 2005, a day after the first anniversary of Bill's death, Karen renewed her vows as a formal devotee of Avatar Adi Da Samraj. She writes:

I started using the room where Bill died, and where we did the three-day vigil over his body, as a meditation hall. And in the year since Bill's death, I haven't missed a day of meditation in that hall, except for the days when I've been traveling—and even then I always meditate and study Adi Da's Teaching. And during that time I have really felt Adi Da's Love and Blessings in my life, and a real strengthening of my relationship with Him. It hasn't even been so much of a strengthening—it's as if the time when I haven't been actively involved in the Way of Adidam has vanished, as if there is no time or space in my relationship with my Guru. And I wanted to thank Him in some way for His Gifts to Bill and me and my family, and it became obvious that renewing my vow of eternal devotion to Him as His devotee was the best gift I could give Him.

The Doctor's Prayer

my mother's death transition, Blessed by Avatar Adi Da

by Ulla Brust, MD
Germany

In August 2003, my seventy-eight-year-old mother had a stroke. For the first few days after the stroke, she wasn't able to speak, but she had outer awareness and could communicate by gestures.

A few days later, she had a second stroke. She was completely paralyzed and, it seemed, without outer awareness—sometimes she reacted with her eyes when someone spoke to her and sometimes she didn't. Soon, she was in a coma, with no signs of possibly recovering, and was put on a feeding tube. I am a medical doctor, and I knew that there wasn't anything that modern medicine could do to reverse her condition.

Several times we thought she would die—her breathing became irregular, with long stops, and it seemed she was struggling for every breath. This lasted for hours, or even a whole day, and then her breathing became normal again.

I have two brothers and two sisters. We all felt that our mother was full of fear—that she was struggling with something and was afraid to die. Each of us told her what we felt moved to tell her in order to help her let go.

The Doctor's Prayer

I also did the laying on of hands. She seemed to be more relaxed when I did this but, later, her face resumed its fearful expression.

In November, difficulties arose with the artificial nutrition, and it became obvious she would die in the foreseeable future. I spent one week with her. Mostly, I sat at her bed and invoked Adi Da, or read passages from His Wisdom-Teaching on the death transition from His book *Easy Death*, or did the laying on of hands. My mother did not know about my Heart-Master: she had been a Catholic, but had not been very religious.

After a week, during which her condition did not change, I had to leave, because I had to go back to work. I still had the feeling that she was afraid to go.

On my last day with her, I had a vision: I saw Avatar Adi Da holding His hands in a Blessing-Gesture. When I arrived at home—about four hundred kilometers from the hospital—I had received an email through the Adidam intranet, explaining how to participate in Avatar Adi Da's "Blessing Puja" for devotees and their families or other intimates. I remembered the vision of Adi Da—the Blessing-Gesture at my mother's bed—and I knew that I should ask Him to Bless her.

At that point, I was totally horrified about my mother's situation. I felt helpless as her daughter.

And I could not help her as a doctor—in her state, no doctor in the world could do anything for her.

Thus, it was so freeing when I realized that there was a possibility of doing <u>something</u> for my mother—I could bring her and her situation to the attention of the Divine Person.

I wrote Avatar Adi Da, asking Him for His Help:

Beloved Lord Adi Da Samraj,
   Divine Heart-Master, may You, by Your Grace, Bless my mother's death process. May she be able to go beyond fear,

to release all resistance, to abandon her body easily—may she be able to surrender to Light itself. Beloved Guru, I cannot thank You enough for Your Help in such a situation. Without You and Your Divine Teaching concerning the process of dying, I would feel totally helpless and shocked and lost in emotional reactivity.

With love and gratitude, Your devotee,
Ulla Brust

I sent the letter with my mother's photo to my Heart-Master.

I left my mother on Friday, and sent in the prayer Saturday. My mother died the following Monday.

I was not present myself but my sister and one of my nephews were with her. They told me that she died very peacefully.

Later, I heard that Avatar Adi Da Blessed my mother the day that she had died.

The night after my mother's death I had a dream. I saw her for a few moments—she came towards me and embraced me silently. After that dream, I knew she was in peace.

❖ ❖ ❖

I have been so grateful for the incredible Gift of being able to turn directly to my Heart-Master in this situation. And it has touched me deeply to feel Avatar Adi Da's Love for everyone. My mother has not been a devotee, but He Blesses all beings.

I recognized, too, that in the past I avoided a direct relationship with Beloved Adi Da. After the experience with His Blessing Puja, I felt the deep desire to be closer to my Beloved Guru. A few months later, I decided to apply for a service retreat* at Adidam Samrajashram. A few months after that, I went on retreat. And during my retreat in His physical Company, I understood even more profoundly that, as His devotee, my devotional relationship to Avatar Adi Da <u>is</u> the practice of the Way of the Heart.

I bow down at His Divine Feet in gratitude.

---

*Devotees of Avatar Adi Da regularly engage periods of retreat in His physical Company or at the Sanctuaries He has empowered. A "service retreat" involves both devotional practices and intensively assisting with a specific project during that time period.

I Am in a Very Good Place Now

profound Help and Blessing during my husband's nine years with Alzheimer's disease, and during his death

by Eileen Mulvihill
Northern California

There are many Sacred Guilds in the cooperative culture of Adidam, including the Mate Moce Guild, which serves devotees and their families in preparing for death and in making the death transition itself.* I am a member of that Guild, and have served many members of my family and several friends during the death process.

When, in 1995, my husband of forty-two years, Joe Mulvihill, was diagnosed with Alzheimer's disease, Avatar Adi Da Samraj was notified. (Joe was not a practitioner of the Way of Adidam, but he was very supportive of my involvement.) Adi Da sent His Love and Blessings over the nine years that I served Joe during his illness. And He sent His Love and Blessings when Joe died, on November 7, 2003. And He sent His Love and Blessings after Joe's death. He Instructed us, He Guided us, and He healed our breaking hearts.

---

*For more about the Mate Moce Guild and Avatar Adi Da's Wisdom about the death process, please see *Easy Death* (Middletown, Calif.: The Dawn Horse Press, 2005).

I had already helped my sister as she went through the ordeal of her husband's Alzheimer's. I had no illusions that this was going to be easy. So, in the beginning of Joe's illness, I engaged the Devotional Prayer of Changes, asking Adi Da Samraj to Bless me with patience and the ability to stay in the disposition of love. I also prayed that Joe and I would somehow, at some level, be able to communicate with each other. All my prayers were answered.

As Joe's illness advanced, he would babble with words I'd never heard before and I would respond as if I understood. If I would just stay calm and listen carefully, eventually he would come out with a word that was a "clue", and I could sense what it was he wanted to say. I could answer him appropriately, and he would register pleased satisfaction.

In 1999, Joe went into a nursing home. It was an all-day trip to visit him, as I couldn't find a nursing home nearby. I spent the two-hour drive there, through beautiful farmland, listening to Adi Da's Teaching on tape. By the time I reached the nursing home I was immersed in Adi Da's Heart-Word, feeling grateful and happy. When I would enter Joe's room I would feel Adi Da's Presence, surrounding me, and surrounding Joe. We would walk in the garden, dance to music, sing together, work on art projects, and I would read to him. My time with him was very special and enjoyable.

❖ ❖ ❖

I knew that Avatar Adi Da was transforming Joe, who was a very serious and reserved man for most of his life. There were many incidents that demonstrated this transformation that Joe was undergoing.

Everyone at the nursing home staff and residents loved him because he was calm and happy (especially Magdalena, a patient with Alzheimer's who was from Spain).

One day when we were painting pictures with magic markers, Magdalena joined us in our art project. I was praising Joe for his work, and put my arm around his shoulder. Magdalena gave me a little push and said, "Mi esposo!" [My husband!]

I Am in a Very Good Place Now

"Ok, Ok!" I said. I had learned firsthand not to argue with an Alzheimer's person. I was happy that Joe had people around him that loved him. Magdalena and Joe had conversations that only they understood.

A week later, when I visited him again, Magdalena poked her head in the door and said to Joe, "Hi, honey." Joe turned to me and said, "Do I know her?" Every visit with Joe produced laughter and humor.

Of course, Joe didn't seem to know me, either. But he liked me! At some level, at some times, I felt he did know me. And I never felt like he "wasn't there".

But one day when I arrived at his room he wasn't there—literally. I asked the nurse's assistant where he was. She said he was in the big recreation hall playing the piano.

"Joe doesn't play the piano," I said.

"Yes he does," she said.

"No, he doesn't," I insisted.

"Follow me!" she said.

When we walked into the hall, Joe was playing the piano. It's true he was only playing with one finger, but he was playing the tune, "Five Foot Two, Eyes of Blue"—perfectly. So I sat down beside him and added the chords, and we had great fun.

Whenever I left, I would always tell him, "I love you, Joe." And he would always say, "I love you, too."

What I observed was that Joe, my very intellectual, computer-nerd husband, who in forty years of marriage had only managed to tell me (maybe) five times that he loved me, was now in his feeling being. It seemed like his left brain had stepped back and his right brain had stepped forward.

He was doing things he had never done before—art, music, expressing his feelings. I feel certain that Adi Da Samraj was purifying Joe of lifetimes of karma.

One day I read him a children's book by Adi Da Samraj: *What, Where, When, How, Why, and <u>Who</u> To Remember To Be Happy*.

When I read him the part that talked about death—about "going to sleep forever"—I noticed a change of expression on his face. I asked him, "Joe, are you afraid of dying?"

He hadn't spoken one understandable sentence all day. But now, in perfect clarity, he said, "No, I am in a very good place now." He wasn't talking about the nursing home. He was bright and happy when he spoke, and I could feel Avatar Adi Da Samraj in the room.

Joe died at 4:55 PM, November 7, 2003, in the most peaceful and easeful manner.

I received a call one morning from the nursing home, telling me that Joe was failing rapidly and I should come. Avatar Adi Da was informed immediately, and I requested His Blessings for Joe.

One of my housemates, Ellen, went with me. When we arrived, Joe seemed to be having trouble breathing and was being given oxygen.

The nursing staff moved Joe's roommate to another room to give us privacy. We started preparing. After straightening up the room, we placed flowers and a photograph of Avatar Adi Da on the table at the foot of his bed. We placed a CD player on the side table and inserted a peaceful devotional chant.

That first afternoon and night, Ellen and I took turns reading Avatar Adi Da's Teaching aloud to Joe, meditating, and engaging the laying on of hands. We also took turns resting and sleeping, so we could serve Joe continuously throughout the night.

The next day my stepdaughter arrived. And even though she and I had talked about, and agreed on, Joe's funeral arrangements when he entered the nursing home—there would be no embalming, the body would be undisturbed for three days at the funeral home before cremation, and I would be able to have a private vigil there—she was having second thoughts. She seemed upset and concerned about the plans. I understood that people express their grief in different ways, and also understood this needed to be resolved. Through the Devotional Prayer of Changes, this occurred Gracefully.

It took four days for Joe to die. I remembered that Joe's process was in Adi Da's Sphere, not mine. I decided to give up my plans, have trust and faith, and surrender the process to Him.

I noticed that when my stepdaughter sat next to Joe and held his hand, he smiled the first smile we had seen since we arrived. She had only visited Joe once or twice in the nursing home. Now she and her husband and her grown children were having a reunion. And even though Joe could not speak, I knew this was exactly what he needed before he could peacefully leave this world.

Then Joe's daughter-in law arrived, and, as it turned out, she became a catalyst to help my stepdaughter and me come to a happy agreement about Joe's final arrangements.

A one-time practicing doctor, Joe's daughter-in-law had given up her practice due to an allergy to surgical gloves. Now she was the host of her own TV show, answering medical questions and interviewing people who were contributing to better health. When she arrived, she basically started interviewing me about the Way of Adidam. My stepdaughter was sitting there listening. At last, I had an opportunity to talk to both of them about Adi Da and Adidam. Joe's daughter-in-law asked questions about the Teaching, the community, the "founder", and our way of life. She asked about our practices regarding marriage, sex, and the care of children.

"What about the ritual you perform at death?" she asked.

As I answered her questions, I felt Adi Da's Presence. I was so completely happy. I thought of all the years I had been involved in Avatar Adi Da's Teaching and had tried to interest my children and stepchildren in this Teaching that was the most important aspect of my life. This was indeed a Blessing.

As a result, my stepdaughter came to understand and gain respect for why it was important to me to follow Adi Da's Instructions about death and dying. We came to a happy agreement, and compromised on one or two issues.

Just before Joe died on Friday, my stepdaughter left on an errand. The doctor came in to check on Joe.

"It won't be long now," he said.

I closed the curtains around the bed and performed laying on of hands from Joe's feet to his head, while chanting "Surrender the body into the life-current," which are Instructions from Adi Da's book on death and dying, *Easy Death*.

Joe's breath became soft, smooth, and easy. Then he just stopped breathing. I waited a while to see if he would start breathing again, but he didn't, so I checked his pulse, but there was none. Then there was a soft gurgling sound. I stood there a few more moments looking at his face—and suddenly his head disappeared in light . . . and all I could see was this bright light. Then the whole body was only light. And the room was only light.

"I am hallucinating," I said to myself. Then the body reappeared.

Then, as if Adi Da was saying, "Do you doubt me?", the head disappeared again into light . . . and the whole body . . . and the whole room. I felt Avatar Adi Da's Spiritual Presence, and I also felt that Joe was gone. I felt the vigil had occurred and that the Blessing had been more than perfect.

After the nurse in charge was called to confirm Joe's death, I had two hours alone with the body to meditate.

My stepdaughter returned, and the funeral home driver arrived and took the body to the funeral home, where it would be undisturbed for three days. We were welcome to sit with the body as much as we desired.

It was dark when my stepdaughter and I left the nursing home. She pointed up to the sky at the full moon and said, "Isn't it beautiful?"

"Yes, more than beautiful!" I agreed.

She had no idea that the full moon, to me, was a sacred symbol—for me, it is a reminder of the Divine Source of all beings.*

---

*In the yearly cycle of celebrations in the Way of Adidam, the full moon in July is an occasion on which devotees of Avatar Adi Da celebrate Him as their Divine Guru, the Avataric Incarnation of the Divine Self-"Brightness".

All through Joe's illness, I felt informed and Blessed by Adi Da Samraj—through His written Word, through the community of His devotees, and through His very Person and the relationship He offers to me and everyone. Because of my Beloved Adi Da Samraj, being Joe's caretaker had become an enjoyment rather than an ordeal.

I saw that Joe, too, was also given profound Help and Blessing. Month by month, over the nine years of the Alzheimer's process, I saw Joe transformed from a fearful, angry person at the beginning of his illness, to a calm, peaceful, and even humorous person, who peacefully transitioned out of this realm into the Divine Embrace of the "Bright" Spiritual Presence of Avatar Adi Da Samraj.

In September 2004, Eileen Mulvihill was on a meditation retreat in Adidam Samrajashram, and had the opportunity to ask Adi Da a question about the death process. What follows is a transcript of her conversation with Avatar Adi Da.

EILEEN MULVIHILL: Beloved Avatar Adi Da, thank you so much for this opportunity to ask You a question. You have given us everything, and one of the Gifts You have given us is Your Wisdom-Instruction regarding death and dying. Over the years as Your devotee, I have been Graced to participate in Your Blessing of the transition of my mother, my father, my brother-in-law, as well as my beloved daughter-in-law, Cathy Lewis, and Tamara, my friend, and most recently, my husband, Joe.

Through those experiences of serving their death and dying process, I resorted to You—and through Your Blessing-Grace, I feel I was instructed regarding my own coming process. My question is about that. But I want to thank You so profoundly for especially Your Help during Joe's transition. I served him for nine years, as his caretaker, the last four years in a nursing home. Whenever I was with him, I felt You there—working with him, serving him, and transforming him. And I am so grateful for this experience. It became an enjoyment to serve Him because of You, and because of Your Wisdom. Thank You.

My question is, if I were to die tomorrow, even though I am still a beginner in my practice, would I still be able to resort to You, find You, and be connected to You?

AVATAR ADI DA SAMRAJ: What is the source of this question? Why would you doubt it?

EILEEN: Sometimes I indulge in self-doubt.

AVATAR ADI DA SAMRAJ: You locate Me, resort to Me now, don't you?

EILEEN: Yes, I do. Thank You.

AVATAR ADI DA SAMRAJ: So then, same.

EILEEN: [whispers] Thank You.

AVATAR ADI DA SAMRAJ: The more mature your practice of the Way of Adidam becomes, the more profound it becomes, the more in-depth it becomes, then the more you will bring to the death process and the less you will indulge in doubts about it. But, nonetheless, beginner or not, you are able to resort to Me now. And that is not going to be taken away just because of a trivial activity like death. [Avatar Adi Da laughs.]

The death process introduces profundities of experience that may not be in your sphere of experience day to day, because of your relative immaturity in practice. Whereas in the case of someone more advanced in the practice of the Way of Adidam, these profundities might be more familiar in advance.

In the death process, your resort to Me remains—throughout all the preliminaries to the actual death transition (while you are still bodily aware). Then, as the in-depth profundities of the death process appear, you will immediately find yourself equipped to enter into Communion with Me on that basis.

So, there is no question about your being able to resort to Me and find Me and enter into Communion with Me during the death process—if you turn to Me, as you do now. What the process after death becomes—where the death transition leads in the domain of possibilities or beyond—is a matter of the maturity of your practice, but it is not a matter of damnation. Yes, you will be filed into the appropriate order of the universe, where you reasonably fit and where things are reasonably familiar to you—but still in terms of Communion with Me.

Death is not about whether or not you will be able to enter into Communion with Me. There should be no doubt of that, and you will discover in the death process that there is no reason to doubt it. The process—in terms of the appearance and association of things to come—is governed by the present lifetime's habits of orientation, disposition and desires, the associations that you cling to (or prefer).

If the Spiritual process is greatly mature and most profound, then it is simply that there are potentials of destiny—or of the transcending of destiny itself—that exceed those that belong to a more limited, conventional disposition. But that is simply a matter of potential and of ultimacy, within the greater scheme of things. If you are right, and given over to Me in your disposition, you will be associated, beyond the death process, with dimensions that are appropriate to your disposition and that are positive in their nature. And that destiny can be changed, through sadhana (or Spiritual practice). There are many planes of potential within the conditional worlds and where the subtler characteristics of the apparent beings settle is different, according to the disposition or degree and nature of Spiritual Realization characterized by the individual while alive.

And if Realization is Most Perfect, then, Divine Translation* replaces continuation in the cosmic realms. So, your continued sadhana always deals with those possibilities. But, once you have entered into the practice of being My devotee, there is no question of it being taken away or becoming lost in the death process. This is fundamental, then, to the death process for My devotee. You are Graced with this opportunity, and fully welcomed by Me to make use of it in that time. So, there is no need to be concerned about it.

EILEEN: Yes, Beloved. Thank You, Beloved. All praise to You, Beloved. I love You so much. Thank You.

AVATAR ADI DA SAMRAJ: Tcha.†

—September 4, 2005

---

*"Divine Translation" is Avatar Adi Da's term for the final demonstration of Divine Enlightenment.
†Avatar Adi Da's characteristic sound of Blessing.

Avatar Adi Da Samraj Blessing Prasad for devotees.
The Mountain Of Attention Sanctuary, 2005

Requesting the Compassionate Blessing of Avatar Adi Da Samraj

> *I do not Serve a "public" role, and I do not Work in a "public" (or even a merely "institutionalized") manner. Nevertheless—now, and forever hereafter—I <u>constantly</u> Bless <u>all</u> beings, and this <u>entire</u> world, and the <u>total</u> cosmic domain.*
>
> —Avatar Adi Da Samraj

Avatar Adi Da Samraj has Compassionately offered to Bless His formal devotees, and their friends and loved ones. Requests for Blessing can be, and are, for any life-situation or circumstance—a health problem, a business situation, an imminent death, or a desire for more profound practice of the God-Realizing Way of Adidam.

If a devotee requests Avatar Adi Da's Blessing for a friend or loved one, that individual must be open and willing to receive His Blessing, and must give their permission for the request to be made.

To initiate a request for Blessing, the devotee writes a devotional letter to Avatar Adi Da, requesting His Blessing. Accompanying the letter is a photograph of the devotee, and of anyone for whom he or she is requesting Blessing. After a Blessing request has been reviewed and approved by the Ruchira Sannyasin Order and the medical staff, the request will be offered to Beloved Adi Da. He is read the letter, and receives the photographs, on a tray adorned with flowers. He may ask questions about the situation, He may verbally send His "Love and Blessings" to one or more of the individuals involved in the Blessing request. And He may Anoint the photographs with Blessing Water, in a mysterious process of Compassionate Divine Baptism.

LOVE AND BLESSINGS

The photos and flowers may then be sent to the "Sukra Kendra", a Holy Temple used only by Avatar Adi Da for the sake of His world-Blessing-Work. At some point, He may ask a devotee to remove them from the Temple, at which point the flowers are dried, and both flowers and photographs are given to the individual who requested His Blessing.

For information about becoming a formal devotee of Adi Da Samraj, please contact your local Adidam center. (See listing on p. 236.)

The Mountain Of Attention Sanctuary, 2005

AN INVITATION

Become a Formal Devotee of Avatar Adi Da

In the depth of every human being, there is a profound need for answers to the fundamental questions of existence. Is there a God? What is beyond this life? Why is there suffering? What is Truth? What is Reality?

In this book, you have been introduced to the Work and Person of Avatar Adi Da Samraj, Who truly and completely addresses all of these fundamental questions. How can Avatar Adi Da resolve these fundamental questions? Because He speaks, not from the point of view of the human dilemma, but directly from the unique Freedom of His Divine State. Adi Da's Birth in 1939 was an intentional embrace of the human situation, for the sake of Revealing the Way of Divine Liberation to all, and Offering the Spiritual Blessing that carries beings to that true Freedom. He is thus the fulfillment of the ancient intuitions of the "Avatar"—the One Who Appears in human Form, as a direct manifestation of the Unmanifest Reality.

Through a twenty-eight-year process of Teaching-Work (beginning in 1972), Avatar Adi Da established the Way of Adidam—the Way of the devotional and Spiritual relationship to Him. In those years of Teaching, He spoke for many hours with groups of His devotees—always looking for them, as representatives of humanity, to ask all of their questions about God, Truth, Reality, and human life. In response, He Gave the ecstatic Way of heart-Communion with Him, and all the details of how that process unfolds. Thus, He created a new tradition, based on His direct Revelation (as Avatar) of the Divine Reality—the Way of Adidam.

In the course of His years of Teaching and Revelation, Avatar Adi Da put into writing all the details of the Way of Adidam in order to make His Divine Wisdom-Teaching available to all in perpetuity. Avatar Adi Da has now gathered together His Avataric Divine Wisdom-Teaching in the many "Source-Texts" which He has designated as His Eternal Communication to humankind. He describes these "Source-Texts" as "True-Water-Bearers", or "Bearers of the 'True Water' of the 'Bright' Divine Reality Itself".

Avatar Adi Da has grouped His "Source-Texts" into twenty-three "Streams", or "Courses". Each of these "Courses" conveys a particular aspect of His Avataric Divine Wisdom-Teaching—and each "Course" (other than the first) may, in principle, include any number of "Source-Texts". These Texts present, in complete and conclusive detail, His Divine Revelations, Confessions, and Instructions.

Avatar Adi Da Samraj does not offer you a set of beliefs, or even a set of Spiritual techniques. He simply Offers you His Revelation of Truth as a Free Gift. If you are moved to take up His Way, He invites you to enter into an extraordinarily deep and transformative devotional and Spiritual relationship to Him. On the following pages, we present a number of ways that you can choose to deepen your response to Adi Da Samraj and consider becoming His formal devotee.

To find Avatar Adi Da Samraj is to find the Very Heart of Reality—tangibly felt in your own heart as the Deepest Truth of Existence. This is the great mystery that you are invited to discover.

Adidam is not a conventional religion.
Adidam is not a conventional way of life.
Adidam is about the transcending of the ego-"I".
Adidam is about the Freedom of Divine Self-Realization.

Adidam is not based on mythology or belief.
Adidam is a "reality practice".
Adidam is a "reality consideration", in which the various modes of egoity are progressively transcended.

Adidam is a universally applicable Way of life.
Adidam is for those who will choose It, and whose hearts and intelligence fully respond to Me and My Offering.
Adidam is a Great Revelation, and It is to be freely and openly communicated to all.

—Avatar Adi Da Samraj

Become a Formal Devotee of Avatar Adi Da

For what you can do next to respond to Avatar Adi Da's Offering, or to simply find out more about Him and the Way of Adidam, please use the information given in the following pages.

Contact an Adidam center near you for courses and events
(p. 236)

Order other books and recordings by and about Avatar Adi Da Samraj
(pp. 237–43)

Visit our website: www.adidam.org
(p. 244)

For young people: Join the Adidam Youth Fellowship
(p. 245)

Support Avatar Adi Da's Work and the Way of Adidam
(p. 245)

LOVE AND BLESSINGS

Contact an Adidam center near you

■ To find out about becoming a formal devotee of Avatar Adi Da, and for information about upcoming courses, events, and seminars in your area:

AMERICAS
12040 North Seigler Road
Middletown, CA 95461 USA
1-707-928-4936

PACIFIC-ASIA
12 Seibel Road
Henderson
Auckland 1008
New Zealand
64-9-838-9114

AUSTRALIA
P.O. Box 244
Kew 3101
Victoria
**1800 ADIDAM
(1800-234-326)**

EUROPE-AFRICA
Annendaalderweg 10
6105 AT Maria Hoop
The Netherlands
31 (0)20 468 1442

THE UNITED KINGDOM
PO Box 20013
London, England
NW2 1ZA
0845-330-1008

INDIA
Shree Love-Ananda Marg
Rampath, Shyam Nagar Extn.
Jaipur–302 019, India
91 (141) 2293080

EMAIL:
correspondence@adidam.org

■ For more contact information about local Adidam groups, please see **www.adidam.org/centers**

Order other books and recordings by and about Avatar Adi Da Samraj

■ ADI DA
The Promised God-Man Is Here

The biography of Avatar Adi Da from His Birth to present time. Includes a wealth of quotations from His Writings and Talks, as well as stories told by His devotees. 358 pp., **$16.95**

■ ADIDAM
The True World-Religion Given by the Promised God-Man, Adi Da Samraj

A direct and simple summary of the fundamental aspects of the Way of Adidam. 196 pp., **$16.95**

■ ADI DA AND ADIDAM
The Divine Self-Revelation of the Avataric Way of the "Bright" and the "Thumbs"

A brief introduction to Avatar Adi Da Samraj and His Unique Spiritual Revelation of the Way of Adidam. 64 pp., **$3.95**

■ THE KNEE OF LISTENING

The Divine Ordeal Of The Avataric Incarnation Of Conscious Light

The Spiritual Autobiography Of The Ruchira Avatar, Adi Da Samraj

The Knee Of Listening was first published in 1972, and has sold more than 100,000 copies, in several editions. The latest edition, published in 2004, contains more than 250 pages of new material, including Essays on the Spiritual Masters who served Adi Da Samraj in His process of Divine Re-Awakening, the secrets of Adi Da's "pre-history" (before His birth), and the unprecedented Events of "Yogic Death" that followed His Re-Awakening in 1970.

From the day I first encountered the writings of Adi Da Samraj (as Da Free John) in the mid-80s, I knew I was reading a contemporary religious genius. . . . In my opinion, the total corpus of Adi Da's Source-Texts, including The Knee Of Listening, *constitutes the most doctrinally thorough, the most philosophically sophisticated, the most culturally challenging, and the most creatively original literature on radical non-duality currently available in the English language.*
—from the foreword by **JEFFREY KRIPAL, PhD**
J. Newton Rayzor Professor of Religious Studies, Rice University
author, *Kali's Child*

822 pp., **$24.95**

■ EASY DEATH

Spiritual Wisdom on the Ultimate Transcending of Death and Everything Else

by Adi Da Samraj

This new edition of *Easy Death* is thoroughly revised and updated with:

- ■ New Talks and Essays from Avatar Adi Da on death and ultimate transcendence
- ■ Accounts of profound Events of Yogic Death in Avatar Adi Da's own Life
- ■ Stories of His Blessing in the death transitions of His devotees

. . . an exciting, stimulating, and thought-provoking book that adds immensely to the ever-increasing literature on the phenomena of life and death. But, more important, perhaps, it is a confirmation that a life filled with love instead of fear can lead to ultimately meaningful life and death.

Thank you for this masterpiece.

—**ELISABETH KÜBLER-ROSS, MD**
author, *On Death and Dying*

544 pp., **$24.95**

NEW FROM THE DAWN HORSE PRESS—

■ THE MUMMERY BOOK

A Parable Of The Divine True Love, Told By Means Of A Self-Illuminated Illustration Of The Totality Of Mind

by Adi Da Samraj

A "prose opera" that shatters the conventional limits of language and raises literary portrayal to radical levels of consciousness.

If Dylan Thomas and Buddha shared a soul, The Mummery Book *is what I would expect from such a joining.*
—**ROBERT BOLDMAN**
The Alchemy of Love

Adi Da makes words crackle and swoon, pound and console with an endless suggestiveness guided by a desire to open up the reader's heart and imagination to the possibility of transformation. . . . The Mummery Book *is an absolutely unique literary occasion.*
—**PHILIP KUBERSKI, PhD**
Wake Forest University

288 pages
hardcover **$29.95**, paperback **$19.95**

■ **MY "BRIGHT" WORD**
by Adi Da Samraj

New Edition of the Classic Spiritual Discourses originally published as *The Method of the Siddhas*

In these Talks from His early Teaching Years, Avatar Adi Da gives extraordinary Instruction on the foundation of true Spiritual life, covering topics such as the primary mechanism by which we are preventing the Realization of Truth, the necessary foundation for Spiritual life, and the function of the Spiritual Master in relation to the devotee.

In modern language, this volume teaches the ancient all-time trans-egoic truths. It transforms the student by paradox and by example. Consciousness, understanding, and finally the awakened Self are the rewards. What more can anyone want?

—**ELMER GREEN, PhD**
Director Emeritus, Center for Applied Psychophysiology, The Menninger Clinic

544 pp., **$24.95**

■ **What, Where, When, How, Why, and Who To Remember To Be Happy**
by Adi Da Samraj

As long as you go on feeling this Mystery, you feel free and full and happy—and you feel and act free and full and happy to others. This is the secret of being happy from the time you are small until the time you are old. —Avatar Adi Da Samraj

A unique Spiritual text for children (of all ages) that leads them through the contemplation of who we are, what we know, what death is, and what true happiness is. 21 full-color illustrations.

hardcover, 48 pages
$14.95 (This book is also available on CD.)

■ THE ADIDAM REVELATION DISCOURSES ON DVD

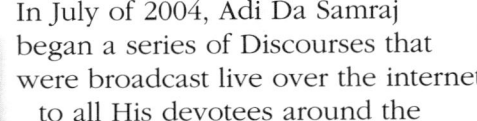

In July of 2004, Adi Da Samraj began a series of Discourses that were broadcast live over the internet to all His devotees around the world. During these remarkable occasions, Adi Da Samraj answered questions from those who were present in the room with Him, but also from devotees in other parts of the world via speakerphone. The "Adidam Revelation Discourse" DVDs offer you the opportunity to see and hear Avatar Adi Da speak in these unique and intimate occasions of Divine Instruction to His devotees. Current available titles include:

■ Transcend the Self-Knot of Fear

Running time: 60 minutes
Includes subtitles in English, Spanish, French, German, Dutch, and Polish.

■ The Divine Is Not the Cause

Running time: 72 minutes
Includes subtitles in English, Spanish, French, German, Dutch, Finnish, Polish, Czech, Chinese, Japanese, and Hebrew.

■ Cracking the Code of Experience

Running time: 86 minutes
Includes subtitles in English, Spanish, German, Dutch, Polish, Czech, Chinese, Japanese, and Hebrew.

DVD
$26.95 each.

■ THE LIBERATING WORD OF AVATAR ADI DA

A Selection of Talks Celebrating 30 years of Avatar Adi Da's Divine Teaching-Revelation, 1972–2002

A collection of nine excerpts from Talks given by Avatar Adi Da, exemplifying some of the principal facets of His Wisdom-Teaching—including "radical" understanding of the ego, the devotional relationship to the Spiritual Master, the lesson of life, the true nature of Real God, a criticism of scientific materialism, His Divine Self-Confession, and more.

Spoken Word CD
Running time: 70 minutes
$16.95

■ DEATH AND THE PURPOSE OF EXISTENCE

A collection of Talks and Recitations that exemplify Avatar Adi Da's essential Wisdom-Teaching on death. Includes a range of excerpts, taken from throughout the 30 years of Avatar Adi Da's formal Teaching Years, that cover topics such as serving a loved-one's death process, fear of death as the foundation of all seeking, what really happens in the death process, preparing for death through real Spiritual practice in the company of a Realizer, the necessity for understanding and transcending the fear of death, and more.

Spoken Word CD
Running time: 69 minutes
$16.95

To find out about and order other "Source-Texts", books, tapes, CDs, and videos by and about Avatar Adi Da, contact your local Adidam regional center, or contact the Dawn Horse Press at:
1-877-770-0772 (from within North America)
1-707-928-6653 (from outside North America)
Or order online from: **www.dawnhorsepress.com**

Visit our website: www.adidam.org

- **SEE AUDIO-VISUAL PRESENTATIONS** on the Divine Life and Spiritual Revelation of Avatar Adi Da Samraj

- **LISTEN TO DISCOURSES** Given by Avatar Adi Da Samraj to His practicing devotees—
  - Transcending egoic notions of God
  - Why Reality cannot be grasped by the mind
  - How the devotional relationship to Avatar Adi Da moves you beyond ego-bondage
  - The supreme process of Spiritual Transmission

- **READ QUOTATIONS** from the "Source-Texts" of Avatar Adi Da Samraj—
  - Real God as the <u>only</u> Reality
  - The ancient practice of Guru-devotion
  - The two opposing life-strategies characteristic of the West and the East—and the way beyond both
  - The Prior Unity at the root of all that exists
  - The limits of scientific materialism
  - The true religion beyond all seeking
  - The esoteric structure of the human being
  - The real process of death and reincarnation
  - The nature of Divine Enlightenment

- **SUBSCRIBE** to the online Global Ashram Magazine

For young people:
Join the Adidam Youth Fellowship

■ Young people under 21 can participate in the "Adidam Youth Fellowship"—either as a "friend" or practicing member. Adidam Youth Fellowship members participate in study programs, retreats, celebrations, and other events with other young people responding to Avatar Adi Da. To learn more about the Youth Fellowship, call or write:

Vision of Mulund Institute (VMI)
10336 Loch Lomond Road, PMB 146
Middletown, CA 95461
phone: (707) 928-6932
email: vmi@adidam.org
www.visionofmulund.org

Support Avatar Adi Da's Work
and the Way of Adidam

■ If you are moved to serve Avatar Adi Da's Spiritual Work specifically through advocacy and/or financial patronage, please contact:

Advocacy
P.O. Box 204
Lower Lake, CA 95457
phone: (707) 928-4800
email: adidam_advocacy@adidam.org

ABOUT THE EDITOR

Bill Gottlieb was editor-in-chief of *Prevention Magazine Books* and Rodale Books from 1986 to 1995, and is the author of *Alternative Cures* (Rodale, 2000) and several other books. He became a devotee of Avatar Adi Da Samraj in 1990, and is currently the editor of Adidam's public internet magazine (at www.adidam.org), and a writer and editor for the Dawn Horse Press, the publishing division of Adidam. He lives near the Mountain Of Attention Sanctuary of Adidam, in northern California. ■

We invite you to find out more about Avatar Adi Da Samraj and the Way of Adidam

■ Find out about our courses, seminars, events, and retreats by calling the regional center nearest you.

AMERICAS
12040 N. Seigler Rd.
Middletown, CA
95461 USA
1-707-928-4936

THE UNITED KINGDOM
P.O. Box 20013
London, England
NW2 1ZA
0845-330-1008

EUROPE-AFRICA
Annendaalderweg 10
6105 AT Maria Hoop
The Netherlands
31 (0)20 468 1442

PACIFIC-ASIA
12 Seibel Road
Henderson
Auckland 1008
New Zealand
64-9-838-9114

AUSTRALIA
P.O. Box 244
Kew 3101
Victoria
**1800 ADIDAM
(1800-234-326)**

INDIA
Shree Love-Ananda Marg
Rampath, Shyam Nagar Extn.
Jaipur–302 019, India
91 (141) 2293080

EMAIL: **correspondence@adidam.org**

■ Order books, tapes, and videos by and about Avatar Adi Da Samraj.
1-877-770-0772 (from within North America)
1-707-928-6653 (from outside North America)
order online: **www.dawnhorsepress.com**

■ Visit us online:
www.adidam.org
Explore the online community of Adidam and discover more about Avatar Adi Da and the Way of Adidam.